NORMAN MacCAIG
A Study of His Life and Work

Marjorie McNeill has lived in Edinburgh all her life and has worked at various times as a civil servant, English teacher and editorial assistant on the Dictionary of the Older Scottish Tongue. She now concentrates on freelance writing and tutoring. She has written articles for newspapers and magazines, mainly on arts and travel topics and has also written productions for the Edinburgh Festival Fringe (on Norman MacCaig and Robert Louis Stevenson) and for the Edinburgh International Festival (on Neil Gunn).

NORMAN MacCAIG
A Study of His Life and Work

MARJORY McNEILL

**MERCAT
PRESS**

First published in 1996 by Mercat Press
James Thin, 53 South Bridge, Edinburgh EH1 1YS

ISBN 1873644 515

Typeset in Ehrhardt 10/12 point at Mercat Press
Printed in Great Britain by Athenaeum Press Ltd, Gateshead

Dedication

To my good friends Douglas, Hilary, Roan and Jean Irving

Contents

Illustrations

Introduction

In the years from the end of the Second World War to the nineteen eighties, there was in Scotland a considerable flowering of poetic talent, the main poets of the period being Hugh MacDiarmid, Norman MacCaig, Sydney Goodsir Smith, Sorley MacLean, Edwin Muir, Robert Garioch and, later, George Mackay Brown, Edwin Morgan and Iain Crichton Smith.

One of the most famous and outstanding of these poets was Norman MacCaig. He was an Edinburgh man, but had strong links with Scalpay, Harris, and with the Assynt area of the North West Highlands. Nearly all of his poems are set in Edinburgh or Assynt, except for a few in foreign settings, notably New York.

The poetry of Scotland is written in three languages—English, Scots and Gaelic. MacDiarmid, who wrote in both Scots and English, considered Scots to be more expressive than English. Sorley MacLean writes all his poetry in Gaelic. (Later translations have been made into English.) MacCaig, however, wrote his poetry entirely in English.

In 1986 MacCaig won the Queen's Medal for his poetry, an award instituted in 1933 by George V. A major book of his poems, *Collected Poems* was published in 1985 by Chatto and Windus. It contains most of his poetry of the years between 1955 and 1985. A revised version of this, containing later poems, was published in 1990.

His poetry is noted for its brevity and wit, its enormous range of subject matter and for its vivid imagery.

MacCaig was to become a frequent performer at poetry readings in Scotland and beyond, travelling eventually to the United States, Australia and Italy, and his readings, put across in a humorous, throw away style, became very celebrated.

He was also noted as a talker of wit and trenchancy and a skilled arguer. A most gregarious person, he became a focus for writers, particularly poets, and his home was to become a setting for many gatherings of poets and friends. When he worked as writer in residence at Edinburgh University, he helped many young poets with advice and encouragement.

I first came across MacCaig at a poetry reading in Edinburgh in the 1960s and became 'hooked' on his poetry, buying every book as it appeared and attending every public reading I could get to in Edinburgh. I interviewed him in 1980 for a magazine article and shortly thereafter started to interview him more extensively in order to write this book. A considerable amount of the material herein is based on this series of interviews. I also travelled on several occasions to Assynt to obtain background material on the poems.

The aim of the book is (1) biographical, (2) to look at the sources from which the poems have sprung, and their recurring themes, and to give a brief analysis of some of them, and (3) to look at the poetry 'scene' to which MacCaig belonged (particularly as it was in Edinburgh from the late 1940s to the 1980s).

The material is dealt with in chronological order. I have occasionally, however, spoken about poems outwith this restriction, in order to illustrate particular points.

M.McN.

Abbreviations for books of poetry

N.B. Most of the poems referred to in this book are in *Collected Poems* (1990) and are not identified further. Those poems not in *Collected Poems* (1990) are identified by the appropriate abbreviation.

RL	*Riding Lights*, 1955
SS	*The Sinai Sort*, 1957
CG	*A Common Grace*, 1960
RAA	*Round of Applause*, 1962
M	*Measures*, 1965
S	*Surroundings*, 1966
RT	*Rings on a Tree*, 1968
MP	*A Man in My Position*, 1969
WB	*The White Bird*, 1973
WR	*The World's Room*, 1974
TS	*Tree of Strings*, 1977
ES	*The Equal Skies*, 1980
WD	*A World of Difference*, 1983
VO	*Voice Over*, 1988
CP	*Collected Poems*, 1990

Note on the editions of *Collected Poems*

Collected Poems was published first in 1985 and was then republished in 1990. The 1990 version contains all the poems in the 1985 version, plus all the poems in *Voice Over* and fifteen additional poems written since then.

Acknowledgements

I would like to express my thanks to the late Norman MacCaig for allowing me to interview him on several occasions between the years 1981 and 1995. Much of the biographical material in the book is based on these interviews. Thanks also to Chatto and Windus and the late Norman MacCaig for allowing me to quote from MacCaig's poetry in this book.

I would also like to thank the following:

For reading and commenting on the book: Daphne Hamilton and Catherine Kerrigan. For interviews: Roderick Watson, Alasdair Macrae, Sorley MacLean, Dolina MacLennan, the late Jimmy Crichton, Ishbel MacLean, John Herdman, Lorn Macintyre, Valerie Gillies, the late Mrs A.K. MacLeod, John MacInnes, Wilfred Grub, Norman MacAskill, Hazel Goodsir Smith, Peter Gossip and Morag Macleod. For letters including material used in the book: George Mackay Brown and Lannette Kennish. For excerpts from written or broadcast material quoted in this book: BBC Radio Scotland and the BBC Rights Archive, London, including work by Edi Stark, Roderick Watson, William Carrocher and Aly Bain. For extracts from other written material quoted in this book: the *Scotsman*, including work by Julie Davidson, Michael Aitken, the late Sydney Goodsir Smith, David Leigh, Stanley Roger Green; *Schola Regia*, the magazine of the Royal High School, Edinburgh; Alasdair Macrae and Stirling University; Karl Miller, excerpt from *Memoirs of Modern Scotland*, published by Faber & Faber Ltd, 1970; Mary Jane W. Scott for permission to quote from her 'Neoclassical MacCaig' in *Studies in Scottish Literature* X, 3 January 1973, p.137 (quoted with permission of the editor); the estate of Hugh MacDiarmid for the use of 'The Little White Rose' from *The Complete Poems of Hugh MacDiarmid* and Penguin Books Ltd, also for extracts from articles in *Poetry Scotland* and *Voice of Scotland*, and for extracts from *The Company I've Kept*, published by Hutchinson & Co; Nancy Gish and the Macmillan Press Ltd; excerpt from *A Glossary of Literary Terms*, Third Edition, © 1971 by M.H. Abrams, reprinted by permission of Holt, Rinehart and Winston, Inc., USA; the estate of Wallace Stevens, excerpts from *Collected Poems*, published by Faber & Faber Ltd, 1955; the estate of Sydney Goodsir Smith for the quotes from 'Kynd Kittock's Land' and 'The Vision of the Prodigal Son' from his *Collected Poems*, John Calder (Publishers) Ltd., London, reprinted by permission of The Calder Educational Trust, London, Copyright © Sydney Goodsir

Smith, 1965, John Calder (Publishers) Ltd., 1975; Joy Hendry, for permission to publish excerpts from an article by Norman MacCaig, 'My Way of It' in *Chapman* 16, Summer 1976, and also for an excerpt from an article by her in the *Scotsman*; George Mackay Brown for excerpts from articles originally in the *Orcadian* and the *Scotsman*; Ian MacDougall and the Mercat Press; Marjorie Wilson and *The Scots Magazine*; Julie Davidson and the Edinburgh *Evening News*; Billy Connolly, Alastair Clark and Mainstream Publishing; John Schofield and Garret Arts; David Campbell; Derek Bowman; Professor A.T. Tolley; Alistair Moffat of STV; Maurice Lindsay; Alan Bold; Stanley Roger Green; Seamus Heaney; Alasdair Gray; O.K. Harris; W.Y. Tindall; the estate of Edwin Muir, and Erik Frykman. For the use of photographs to: the late Norman MacCaig, Jessie Ann Matthew, Edinburgh University Library, Scotsman Publications Ltd, Michael McNeill, Seán Costello and Gordon Thomson.

1. | Early Life

When Norman MacCaig was a small boy he used to read a tremendous amount. His mother, irritated by his 'nose in a book' approach to things, said to him one day, 'Why do you read so much? Why don't you get your own ideas?'

It seems that he took her advice because he went on later to be noted not just for his academic ability, but for the originality of his vision.

He was born on 14 November, 1910, to Robert McCaig[1] and Joan (née MacLeod), and was given the names Norman Alexander. His father, who came from Haugh of Urr in Dumfriesshire, was a chemist by profession and had a shop at 9 Dundas Street, Edinburgh. His father's father was a carter who came from Argyll. Norman MacCaig's mother had come from Scalpay, Harris, to Edinburgh at the age of 16 to work. They married and set up house at 11 Dundas Street in a tenement flat. Norman was the youngest of four children—the others were Ruby, Ella and Frances.

His father was very much an Edwardian in dress and manner. Tall and distinguished-looking, his habitual dress was a dark suit, tie and wing collar. He dispensed advice and prescriptions along with the occasional bit of witty repartee.

MacCaig's mother was a very lovable person. When she was young she was pretty, with black hair and beautiful violet-coloured eyes. She had a fairly volatile temperament. One minute she would be ticking off one of the children, the next laughing. She used to laugh silently, with tears running down her cheeks. She spoke Gaelic and English but had never been taught to read and write, and according to MacCaig, 'thought in images'.

She did some strange things with words. Of someone who forgot to shut the door, she demanded, 'Who left that door in a peep?' When the daughter of a friend was ill with something wrong with her eyes, she asked her friend, 'Why don't you take her to the eyeopium hospital?'

When still a boy, MacCaig went several times to the island of Scalpay, which lies off Harris, for his holidays. This had been the home of his mother and when he returned there he was surrounded by her relatives. Almost everybody on Scalpay is related by marriage. MacCaig's mother was called Joan or Johan or Seonag (the Gaelic for Joan). People in Harris were always given family names; relatives would be hurt if a child was given a name not already 'in the family'.

The community of about 600 people all lived fairly near each other on the coast.

1

The land was poor, peaty soil, and the people lived by crofting and fishing, using peat for fuel, keeping a cow and growing potatoes in lazy beds (a mixture of peat and seaweed).

At night one climbed into a box bed. This would be built of wood rather like a cupboard and had thick curtains or wooden doors. Built thus to conserve warmth and combat the freezing temperatures of the Highlands, these beds were snug, dark and stuffy.

> Hers was the only house
> where I've lain at night
> in the absolute darkness
> of a box bed, listening to
> crickets being friendly.[2]

As a boy MacCaig fished from the pier and explored the coastline.

> A chugging prawn boat slides round Cuddy Point
> Where in a gale
> I spread my batwing jacket and jumped further
> Than I've jumped since. There's where I used to sail
> Boats looped from rushes. On the jetty there
> I caught eels, cut their heads off and watched them slew
> Slow through the water. Ah—Cape Finisterre
> I called that point, to show how much I knew.[3]

A wrecked boat attracted his attention on one holiday and in the 1950s he wrote a poem about the old hulk and how it had appeared, although wrecked, still to have a life of its own, like a ghost.[4]

The sailors of the Western Isles wrote love songs about being at sea and wanting to be back home with their sweethearts. There would also be humorous songs, often about fishing trips. MacCaig's Uncle Roderick[5] used to take him, when he was aged about 12, out fishing. He admired his uncle very much for his strength and sense of humour and for the fact that he knew many songs. His uncle's boat, called a drifter, trailed out a long net, and when this net was pulled in it glowed under the water with phosphorescence.

One of MacCaig's other uncles, Seamus, was a tweed merchant. MacCaig said of him:

Uncle Seamus was my mother's brother. He wrote a couple of novels in Gaelic. This was 50 years ago. One person who read them would not say if they were any good as novels; but they were enraptured with the use of Gaelic...For a crofter's son, at that time, it was a strange thing.[6]

In fact this particular uncle suffered for a period from insanity:

The poet's parents, Joan and Robert McCaig, in 1956

> Mad on his small island
> he scribbled by lamplight, fluttering down
> great snowflakes of paper
> on to the drift at his feet.[7]

One of MacCaig's best known poems concerns his Aunt Julia.[8] She breezes out at us through the poem—a vibrant person—energetic; speaking Gaelic with a loud voice like a seagull and able, when spinning, apparently to draw yarn out of the air. She used to get angry with MacCaig because he could not answer all her questions— he could not understand a lot of what she was saying.

'Laggandoan, Harris' is also about days on Scalpay as a boy. An artistic poem with a lyrical quality, it concerns a bullock, dragon flies, frogs and grasshoppers, and amongst them all, his cousin Johann, Uncle Roderick's daughter:

> Down from the moor, between two rocks
> The furnace sun has calcined white,
> Johann, humped with a creel of peats,
> Comes leaning forward through the light.

The Free Church of Scotland, which flourishes in Lewis, Harris and Scalpay, is very Calvinist and is against social drinking, dancing and secular singing. MacCaig's parents were not religious people. He grew up an atheist and remained so all his life. As a boy he found the Free Church beliefs irksome and inexplicable. They appeared to him to be very negative. On Sundays the severity was stepped up—people could not even go for a walk. One was supposed to read a good book. He was given a row once for whistling a psalm tune on a Sunday, although he had chosen the tune under the impression that he was being tactful! Not surprisingly, perhaps, poets and Calvinism seldom mix. Sorley MacLean, the Gaelic poet, was once discussing the matter with Hamish Henderson, a specialist on Scottish folklore. Henderson mentioned 'decadent Calvinism' and MacLean remarked that the trouble with Calvinism was that it had not reached its decadence yet!

In MacCaig's young days, the Scalpay people went by sea to the church on Harris. Almost everybody from Scalpay went to the services, young and old. Religion was very much a part of society. A Free Church was established on Scalpay after 1929.

MacCaig has frequent references in his poems to his dislike of the Calvinistic mind with its narrow 'thou shalt not' attitude. Describing a Sunday in the North West of Scotland he relates:

> Up from that mist crowds
> the present. This day has lain long,
> has dozed late, till
> the church bell jerks and, wagging madly
> in its salty tower, sends its voice

clanking through the sabbath drowse.
And dark minds in black clothes gather like
bees to the hive, to share
the bitter honey of the Word, to submit
to the hard judgement of a God
my childhood God would have a difficulty
in recognising.
Ten yards from the sea's surge
they sing to Him beautiful praises
that surge like the sea,
in a bare stone box built
for the worship of the Creator
of all colours and between-colours, and of
all shapes, and of the holiness
of identity and of the purifying light-stream
of reason. The sound of that praise
escapes from the stone box
and takes its place in the ordinary communion
of all sounds, that are
Being expressing itself—as it does in its continuous,
its never-ending creation of leaves,
birds, waves, stone boxes—and beliefs,
the true and the false.[9]

But the people on Scalpay were kindly. In his poem 'Return to Scalpay', written much later in life, MacCaig described how he was overcome by the kindness, warmth and simple sincerity of relatives:

My city eyeballs prickle; it's hard to bear
With such affection and such gaiety.

Scalpay revisited?—more than Scalpay. I
Have no defence,
For half my thought and half my blood is Scalpay,
Against that pure, hardheaded innocence
That shows love without shame, weeps without shame,
Whose every thought is hospitality—
Edinburgh, Edinburgh, you're dark years away.

MacCaig's early experiences on Scalpay were to affect his whole life. His later love of the wild countryside of Assynt stemmed to some extent from memories of childhood on Scalpay, and his interest in animals and nature had been fostered by long days roaming this small remote island and its coastline as a boy. All through his poetry there were to recur acutely observed poems about animals and birds, and his

5

love of the sea, fostered by Uncle Roderick, led him to write many poems about sea voyages and fishing around the coast of Sutherland.

As a schoolboy in Edinburgh, he went first to Broughton School when he was five and then to the Royal High School. Later, in a poem about a man dying in the Calton Jail, opposite the 'Royal High', he described his early days at school:

> My long shanks
> Pelmetted with short trousers,
> Storked me into the school opposite
> Where my long head
> Under its plume of hair
> Sucked in words and choked on mathematics.
>
> From a classroom I looked over
> A smoky valley and Royal Palace
> To a long, curving cliff—
> Samson's Ribs...[10]

The boys ate their meals in the 'Grubby' and conducted their fights in the basements. As MacCaig put it, 'Blue eyed boys went down and black eyed boys came up'.

He disliked the Rector, Mr W. King Gillies, who appears to have been a fairly autocratic figure, much devoted to extolling the virtues of physical fitness, unselfishness and doing what one was told to do. He was very insistent on school uniform, including a cap. MacCaig did not like wearing a hat and so calmly and stubbornly refused to do so. One time the Rector gave him the belt for alleged lateness. MacCaig considered him a bully.

This shows early on what was later to become a theme of some of his work—his dislike of 'authority figures' and his joy in taking them down a peg. He was later to debunk 'religious chaps', academics, certain lady research students, rich New Yorkers, politicians, leaders of men, tourists at religious shrines etc. It also indicated early on an extremely stubborn resistance to doing what he did not want to do. He was later to use this stubborn trait in his refusal to join the Forces during the Second World War which led to a period of incarceration as a conscientious objector.

But he in fact enjoyed his school days. It was a disciplined but happy, hard-working environment. He and the others were exposed to various subjects, including poetry, although Matthew Arnold's 'Sohrab and Rustum' was the most modern poetry they were given. Poetry meant little to him in his early school days. It was just a subject that schoolboys had to suffer. When he was 16, however, his English master, whom he liked very much, and who was known as 'Puggy Grant', gave the boys some homework. They had either to write an essay on some topic or produce a poem. MacCaig wrote a poem because it was shorter. Thereafter several of his poems appeared in the school magazine *Schola Regia* and he won prizes for literary essays.

The first to appear was 'Coronach'.[11] It is a lament for the death of a hero,

Tormod Laidir:

> Oh black was the day! Oh black was the hour!
> Oh curst was the hand that did rob us forever
> Of the life that was dearest, the heart that was best,
> For Tormod Laidir is gone—and for ever!

In Easter, 1928, a poem by MacCaig, with a classical theme, entitled 'To Faunus' appeared and also a poem called 'Noonday Hours':

> ...Slow creep
> From flower to honeyed flower the droning bees
> Along the mossy wall, now buried deep
> With honeysuckle...[12]

In that same year he won the London Royal High School Club Prize for his poem 'Autumn',[13] the Walter Scott Prize, and the Robert Louis Stevenson Club Prize with an essay entitled 'Stevenson the Traveller'.[14]

The Royal High School not only fostered a high standard of literacy, it also went in for stage productions. A series of Gilbert and Sullivan operas were produced when MacCaig was there. He appeared in the chorus of *HMS Pinafore* and sang the part of Nanki Poo one year in *The Mikado*. He got the part not for any acting ability but because he had a good tenor voice and one of the songs goes up to top 'A'. He was the only boy who could sing the note!

> N.A. McCaig did not seem at home in his acting, but his singing was beautiful, and his duet with Yum-Yum (G. A. Smith) was the best piece of singing in the whole production.[15]

He also took up debating when he was in Class VI A, and the Debating Society Notes in *Schola Regia* for Easter 1928 report:

> The last meeting of the session was held on 16th March, the debate, 'That the Barbarian is Happier than the Civilised Man'. The speakers were McCaig for the Affirmative, Stephen for the Negative. They were supported by Murray and Lowdon, the last-named gentleman having an extremely hot time of it in Open Debate.

MacCaig's later love of argument was receiving its baptism at these meetings.

His best subject at school was English but he also liked Classics. He knew that he wanted to become a teacher and some irrational instinct told him that he did not want to teach English; that teaching the subject and marking essays would spoil his pleasure in it. So he decided to study Classics at University, with the intention of becoming a Classics teacher.

His reasons for liking Classics appear to stem from his roots in Gaeldom. The Gaelic language is considered to be very formal and, in this way, similar to Latin and Greek. MacCaig said that his own love of form and formalism, his obsession with the use of rhyme and metre in poetry, was an inbred characteristic deriving from his Gaelic ancestry. He refused to accept the romantic vision of the Gaels sometimes portrayed in literature as 'chaps twangling harps while their ladies are away marrying seals' as he once put it. He saw Gaelic art, literature and music as being very formal; beautiful but not 'romantic' in the disparaging sense of being produced in an impulsive, untidy way. This love of form also extended to his musical taste which embraced Bach, Beethoven, Haydn but rejected 'romantics' like Mendelssohn.

His own poetry is not 'classical' by any means, although it is full of classical allusions. He himself had some of the qualities of the Greeks and Romans in his love of learning, in particular philosophy, poetry, music; and in his questioning mind which refused to accept the opinions of others without examining them under a microscope and invariably finding flaws in them. His was a tenacious mind, a seeking, searching intelligence. He was a free thinker, baffled and perplexed by the riddles of the universe. Above all he hated being labelled and maintained he was simply Norman MacCaig, a man who liked a lot of things including writing poetry. 'I never think of myself as a poet.'

MacCaig won a classical bursary in the school bursary competition in 1928. He then left the Royal High to study Classics for four years at Edinburgh University.

2. University and Early Poetry

It was at Edinburgh University that MacCaig made what he once referred to as his 'final stage appearance' as an actor at the age of 19. The Reader in History appeared in the Classics Library one day and said he proposed producing a play by Aristophanes in Greek called *The Frogs*. MacCaig, who later laid claim to the title 'worst actor in Europe', was given the key part of Dionysus. He knew that he was quite unable to reproduce a performance the same way twice so made no attempt to act well at rehearsals. When he had to faint, for instance, he just lay down.

Fortunately the play was only produced once and into the performance he put all the things he had thought of doing and never done. He was a terrific success!

The play was performed on 28 February 1930, in the hall of the Edinburgh Ladies' College in George Street. The *Scotsman* review of the time read:

...an audience of some 500 people...laughed last night over the production in Greek, by the Edinburgh University Classical Society, of the 'Frogs' of Aristophanes, as heartily, perhaps, as did the Greeks who attended the play's first production in Athens in the year 405 B.C. True, it was not the wit of Aristophanes which they laughed at so much as the slap-stick comedy of the play—the Aristophanic equivalent of the throwing of custard pies, as we have it on the cinema screen in the twentieth century.

...the actors showed very much better mastery of their Greek lines than a good many amateurs show of their English ones...Mr N. A. McCaig, taking the part of Dionysus, had the biggest memory test to come through, and came through it admirably...

A letter to the Editor of *Schola Regia* of Easter, 1930, says of the play:

Handyside (playing Euripides) and McCaig certainly distinguished themselves there, and are to be congratulated, not less on their actual performance, which was second to none in the cast, than on the fact that after a year of Classics at the University they are still sufficiently interested in the subject to undertake such a task. To the outward eye, in fact, the Classical men seem worthy of all pity and sympathy, so harassed is their look, so dry the straw they chew.

But other diversions were at hand. Dancing was a popular activity at the University and MacCaig frequently attended the dances. A writer in the *Student* of 6 February 1929 enthuses:

> Miss Lightbody, gowned exquisitely in a frock of floral design, made an admirable hostess, and was ably seconded by her colleagues, whose gowns were perfectly indescribable (by a mere man).

The ideal female in the 1920s was still wilting, feminine, delicate and mysterious, although a murmur of changes to come was echoing from some of the University women, particularly the women 'medics'.

MacCaig, in fact, met his future wife, Isabel Munro, at a dance at the University. He told Edi Stark about this meeting during a radio interview[1] in 1993.

> She was in English and I was in Classics. The English Society and the Classical Society occasionally had a dance together. I was a hot boy at the jigs and at a dance Isabel was sitting so I asked her up to dance and she turned out to be an extraordinarily good dancer. As I was also. The only thing I can boast about!

Isabel was a small, quiet girl. She was of slight build and fine-featured. She was studying English Literature and was a brilliant student. She was in the same class at University at Sorley MacLean, the Gaelic poet.

In addition to his prowess at dancing, MacCaig appears to have acquired by this time a reputation as an eccentric for his habits of smoking a pipe and playing pibroch.[2] A correspondent called Vercingetorix in *Schola Regia*, Summer 1932, wrote:

> ...A word to the wise! From time to time a pungent odour or a dense pall of smoke, more often than not supplemented by a succession of shrill plaintive notes, presenting a triple phenomenon which does not fail to excite comment among gentlemen of a scientific turn of mind, warns the initiated of the vicinity of MacCaig.

He played on a chanter (not on bagpipes) or on a fiddle. In fact it is physically impossible to play pibroch correctly on the fiddle because of the complicated grace notes. He, however, invented clusters of grace notes that gave something of the effect.[3] He also became very good at playing jigs and reels. He never played in public except perhaps at a small gathering at home.

He always enjoyed listening to bagpipe music, particularly to a single bagpiper playing pibroch.

> The far notes were blaeberries—bubbles
> of blue blood in the dark.
> They clustered towards me, turning red...

J. L. Brown   J. E. McIntyre   A. A. Macneill   N. A. McCaig   E. J. Pretty   T. O. A. Munro

J. G. A. Reith   D. Maxwell   A. E. M. Hogg   Prof. Richmond   Prof. Calder   A. N. Strachan   J. C. Watson

MacCaig's graduation from Edinburgh University, with Honours in Classics, in 1932
(photo courtesy of Edinburgh University Library)

> The piper in the dark walked
> under his own flourish—delicately inserting
> the punctuation and pointing of gracenotes.[4]

The students worked hard and long at their studies in the dusty splendour of Edinburgh University's Old College rooms. The Final Examinations loomed up relentlessly at the end of the fourth year.

> …Watson and McCaig, who have trodden the stony road of classics until they are like to be varicose, are drawn together by the bitter knowledge that in June the road will either take a turning or go over a precipice, and are wont to solace each other with plaintive Gaelic melodies, whistled surreptitiously under the nose of Professor Richmond…[5]

He graduated in June, 1932, with Honours in Classics. In 1932 he went to Moray House[6] for a year. He hated Moray House because he thought the lecturers treated the students like children. Scheduled to attend a class in voice production, he went on the first day and the teacher got them all to open their mouths and then peered into them. 'Fine cavities at the back but tongue-tied' she said of him. After that he skipped the class.

He got a certificate that permitted him to teach in secondary and primary schools, but was not able to find work teaching Classics. There were very few teaching vacancies between 1933 and 1939 and although he applied for four Classics posts in Scotland, he did not get any of them.

In 1933 he was unemployed for nine months and then had a succession of temporary posts, including teaching Latin for a year and a half at Portobello Secondary School. In 1936-7, while he was there, the Art Teacher of that school, George Findlay McKenzie, painted his portrait. It was painted in a studio in Frederick Street, Edinburgh, and was hung in the R.S.S.A. about that time. MacCaig is shown seated and wearing a brown jacket and green trousers. The portrait is a serious one of the poet aged about 26, looking directly at the viewer with a rather hypnotic stare. It was later bought by the University of Edinburgh and now hangs in the School of Scottish Studies.

After leaving Portobello High School, MacCaig always taught in primary schools, the first such post being in Gillespie's Boys' School. Eventually he got a permanent job at Craiglockhart Primary School. He was there when the War broke out in 1939 and he went back there after the War in 1945.

He enjoyed teaching primary school children. He always loved talking and dealing with people whether they were 11, 23, or 60 years old. He maintained that age was irrelevant—that he could not be bored if he was talking to people. He in fact taught happily in various primary schools in Edinburgh for 30 years.

He and Isabel, who was by now an English teacher, were married in 1940 and bought a house in Broughton Street, Edinburgh.

He continued writing poetry after he took up teaching. He had no idea of trying to get anything published and wrote purely for himself. This had a bad effect. The poems became more and more obscure—outpourings of images. They had metre and rhyme because he liked form in poetry and liked experimenting with metres and rhymes and stanzas.

There was a school of French surrealist poetry in the 1930s which influenced some British writers. MacCaig's poems came near to surrealism. The surrealists thought that three quarters of the mind was 'submerged' but that one could capture ideas and fleeting images from this submerged part and express them in a kind of 'dream' writing. All too easily, however, this led to the poet merely writing in streams of unrelated images. There were surrealist artists around at this time— Salvador Dali and Magritte, for example. Surrealism seemed to 'work' in paint, producing shocking and strange, eerie effects, but it did not appear to work in poetry.

MacCaig always wrote a certain amount of very abstract poetry, a lot of which is extremely difficult to follow. It is interesting to note that he had a strong love of music—that most abstract of arts. In fact he said that if he had been able to compose music he would have preferred to do that rather than write poetry. His poetry, whether abstract and obscure or clear and lucid, was always written fairly rapidly and with few corrections, and one can compare this facility with that found in some composers, particularly Mozart and Schubert, of writing music as if it gushes forth from a spring inside the composer.

MacCaig got involved with a group of poets who became known as the 'New Apocalypse Movement'. They also included Tom Scott, Maurice Lindsay and Dylan Thomas. A. T. Tolley, writing in *The Poetry of the Thirties*[7] of this movement said:

> Perhaps the most interesting thing about the Apocalypse movement was that it was a provincial, non-London-Oxford-Cambridge movement...It was also a Celtic movement. Hendry, Scott, Fraser and MacCaig were Scots; Treece was half Welsh. They associated themselves with two established Welsh writers, Dylan Thomas and Vernon Watkins...

They were thought to be influenced by Marx and Freud. They put a lot of stress on individualism and the examination of self, two ideas which in fact persisted in MacCaig's poetry long after he stopped being 'apocalyptic'!

They published their first anthology in 1939, called, fairly predictably, *The New Apocalypse*. A. T. Tolley said of this anthology: 'Norman MacCaig's poems differ little from bad surrealist poetry, except in so far as they seem to aim at a unity of imagery.' Tolley goes on to accuse Henry Treece, one of the leaders of the Movement, of pretentiousness and of bathos and accuses the Movement as a whole of 'the carelessness that goes along with self importance.'

Hugh MacDiarmid poured a salutory shower of cold water on the Movement in the second number of *Poetry Scotland*, 1945, where he wrote:

> The New Apocalypse group is by no means free of the reproach that new literary

movements in England are generally rigged up in the cast-off garments of French and other European experimentalists of some thirty years earlier. The New Apocalypse group largely shares and acts upon the theories of the French Surrealists …These doctrines led in France to some brilliant destructive satire, much amusing nonsense and a little real poetry—but the English, and Scottish, writers of this school have none of the audacious virtuosity, argumentative resources, capacity for abandon, or even the palest reflection of the objurgative and comminatory powers of their European forerunners. They are more apt to achieve a grotesque and dismaying incoherence similar to that in alleged messages 'from beyond the Veil'; and I dislike and disbelieve in Surrealism for the same reason that I dislike and disbelieve in Spiritualism.

However, during the War Isabel sent some of her husband's poems to Routledge and Kegan Paul, and they were published in two books called *Far Cry* (1943) and *The Inward Eye* (1946). MacCaig latterly abhorred these two books of early poetry and told people, 'If you see any of them in people's bookcases, offer to buy them for £10, or steal them, then take them home and burn them!'

It was easy to write obscure poetry. He often found that he did not understand what he had written when he re-read it the next day! In an article called 'My Way of It'[8] written in 1976 he explained:

I said poetry involves order. It has to submit to the control of the rational mind—it's not enough to lift the trap-door to the subconscious and lasso whatever crawls out. I say this, blushing with guilt, for there was a time in the thirties and early forties when that is pretty much what I did. Poem after poem was a splurge of hardly related images, sloppily bound together—and it wasn't enough—only by the blessed formalities of metre and rhyme. An odd thing is that men from Cornwall to Edinburgh (and Glasgow), who didn't know each other or what the others were up to, found themselves writing in this same foolish way. They became known as the New Apocalypse and serve them right. I was rescued by the only critical remark that was ever any use to me, when my second book came out and a friend, having read it, handed it back to me, saying, 'When are you publishing the answers?' This took me several steps back towards my senses and I started on the long haul towards lucidity. Some years later I read, in a novel by Peter de Vries, a nice remark made by a woman to her husband about a friend of theirs: 'He's very profound on the surface but deep down he's shallow', and I greeted that with a fanfare. The label 'Apocalyptic' stuck, as labels do, long after it was contravening the Trades Descriptions Act and even yet I occasionally hear it and am reduced to shuddering fits and grittings of teeth, for it's long since I decided that poems which are wantonly or carelessly obscure (not difficult) are bad art and bad manners.

The New Apocalypse perhaps deservedly collapsed in about 1943 and MacCaig went on to develop a more coherent style.

It is interesting to note that he had some, very tenuous, connections with Dylan Thomas at this stage in that they belonged to the same Movement and had poems published in the same anthologies. MacCaig, in fact, admired the poetry of Thomas. Some years later, in 1948, Dylan Thomas and Dame Edith Evans gave a reading in the Freemasons' Hall, Edinburgh, as part of the official Edinburgh Festival.[9] MacCaig attended this and sat near the middle of the auditorium. The people at the back could not hear Thomas and sent round notes in the interval asking him to speak up. The acoustics of the hall were blamed for this problem. The next day Thomas was in the company of Hector MacIver, an English teacher at the Royal High School. They went drinking. It is probable that some of their time was spent in the well known Milne's Bar on the corner of Hanover Street and Rose Street. Thomas was to do a broadcast. He was drinking rather a lot and people started telling him it was time he stopped and went to the studio. Agreeing to go, he started to leave, and fell flat on his face. He lay there on the floor, lifted his face up and said quite calmly,

'I can't blame that on the acoustics!'

It took MacCaig ten years of writing poetry to haul himself out of the Apocalyptic phase. He still, however, retained some elements of the surreal in his poems.

3. | War Years

In 1939, when MacCaig was teaching at Craiglockhart Primary School, the Second World War broke out. Every able-bodied man between the ages of 18 and 41 was liable for conscription. MacCaig was totally anti-War.

His feelings of pacifism first emerged when, as a child, he read popular illustrated magazines about the First World War. He read these with the kind of interest with which children now watch horror films and he was disgusted by what he saw and read.

Later, the Spanish Civil War also influenced him emotionally as did other international events of the 1930s. There was a feeling that war was coming. But MacCaig was a committed pacifist from a very early age.

He was called up for the Army in the winter of 1941, a winter of heavy and prolonged snow. His parents, on hearing that he did not intend to join up, were much upset.

> My father...thought I was just being a cheeky young man when the letter came. He was very disturbed indeed. He lost his temper. But that was only that morning. After six weeks or so it was totally accepted by both my parents. So that I had an easy journey compared with a lot of young men.[1]

He was summoned before a Tribunal in Edinburgh, where since he was unwilling to join the Regular Army he was instructed to join the Pioneer Corps at Ilfracombe. On being told this he wrote to the Commanding Officer and said he was not coming. As a result he was arrested and placed in the guardhouse at Edinburgh Castle. He found himself with a lot of other men. Most of them were up for 'absence without leave'. MacCaig was the only pacifist. He recalled:

> A big shot—the Commanding Officer in the Castle—came round to inspect us in the guardhouse. Everybody had their beds tidy and their boots in the proper place. I'd just made up mine as if I were at home. In he came. We were all shouted at to 'Stand to attention!' They all sprang to attention. And I didn't. I was sitting on the edge of my bed and I just stayed sitting. The Commanding Officer flushed crimson and started shouting and bawling at me. I said, 'You don't realise I'm not in the Army. I'm a pacifist. They've summoned me to the

Army but I'm not going because I'm a pacifist. I've resigned.' He nearly exploded. I thought he was going to burst. But I didn't get up on my feet.

The rest of the soldiers were astonished. Their opinion of MacCaig suddenly rose. MacCaig: 'I was their lily white boy after that.'

History does not record how the confrontation with the C.O. ended. Shortly after this the men in 'jankers'[2] had their lunch.

Our lunch in the guardhouse was laid on a table and you just piled in—which I wouldn't or couldn't. They just swarmed like bees. And out of that dense mass an arm emerged from this tough guy—and he was a real toughie—handing me something to eat, and this fellow mutters, 'There ye are, chum.' To a 'conshie'![3] Well, this tough guy was on his way to Barlinnie[4] I think for the sixth or seventh time—probably for small offences, absent without leave, that sort of thing. And yet it's he whose arm came out of that mob and handed me my lunch...I was in good favour with them.[5]

In the Second World War the state recognised objections made to military service on philosophical grounds as well as those based on formal religion. MacCaig had said at his Tribunal that he was prepared to go into the R.A.M.C. or the Red Cross, but he was not going to kill people. Since he was prepared to go into the Medical Corps, they could not register him as a conscientious objector, so he was posted to the Non-Combatant Corps which was run by the Pioneer Corps. The Corps sergeant and a private escorted him to Ilfracombe.

His reasons for objecting lay somewhere between morals and ethics. An atheist, he could not claim to object on religious grounds. While other men suffered the tortures of being torn between religious belief and patriotism, MacCaig suffered no such dilemma. He distrusted politicians absolutely whether Communist, Tory, Labour or any other name. He refused point blank to go out and kill other people because someone else told him to do so. 'Why', he put it, 'should I drop a bomb on Hamburg, on people who are just the same as me?'[6]

The N.C.C. was a rather comical section of the Army with a strong 'Dad's Army' flavour about it. They were concerned with such matters as firewatching and patching up country roads. One or two cynics considered that some of the things they had to do probably retarded the War effort rather than helped it. They had to stand a certain amount of abuse from civilians who called them 'yellow bellies'. But the men in the Army never gave MacCaig or his colleagues in the N.C.C. a single insult. The worst they came in for was the odd joke. MacCaig: 'I was once in a train with a lot of soldiers. I had a cap with N.C.C. on it. I was asked by another soldier if it stood for "Norwegian Camel Corps"!'[7]

He caused some trouble in the unit by refusing to do work which supported the War, such as repairing a tank depot and piling up stores in Southampton for the invasion of the continent. As a result, he was court martialled.

If the Army did not believe the person was a conscientious objector, he was sent to a military prison for six months and then returned to his unit. If they did believe him, he was sent to a civilian prison for 93 days and thereafter brought again before the Tribunal and, if they still believed him, they gave him his 'ticket' to go home. He was not then allowed to return to his job but had to do hospital work or land work. The court believed MacCaig and he was put in prison for 93 days—first in Winchester and then in Wormwood Scrubs. MacCaig:

> My recollection of Winchester Prison is that it was full of bed bugs. Every night you went poking with a needle in the holes in the bed frame and the table frame. And the food was atrocious. People who applied to be allowed to work in the garden were allowed to work in the garden. So I did. And if you came across a potato that hadn't been picked last year we ate it raw: not a good idea, but we were very hungry. Most of the talk was about food—not, as you might think, sex. Some of the boys said, 'Oh, you should see the food they have in such and such a prison. My God, it is real good stuff there.' You know, some of them had been in prisons all over the place.[8]

He was in Winchester Prison for about three weeks and then was moved to Wormwood Scrubs which had an easier regime and where the food was excellent.

> We arrived in London to go to Wormwood Scrubs the very day the buzz bombs started operating. And really they were panic stricken. The driver of the van that took us from the station to the prison, oh, he was in a terrible state: 'The war's over! We can't stop them! They've not even got pilots in them! If you shoot them they just fall to the ground and burst anyway!' But they got used to them. It's marvellous what people can stomach.[9]

If he had been feeling guilty he would have hated being in prison but, on the contrary, he felt entirely justified in taking this stand and merely regarded Wormwood Scrubs as a rather grubby 'bed and breakfast' establishment. Most of the others in prison with him were there for religious reasons.

He stood up well to incarceration, drawing on a special defence system to combat stress—a peculiarly Scottish ability in time of trouble to withdraw behind a horny exterior; to become in his own words, 'carapacious and testudinous'. As a result of these experiences, he learned the great lesson that if you take on people in authority they can't make you do what you don't want to do—though they can punish you for it.

While he was away in the army, Isabel had their first child, Joan. She did not tell him about the birth until it was over because she did not want to worry him further while he was involved in the war problems.

They were helped financially by the fact that Edinburgh Education Authority, who had been MacCaig's employer while he was teaching, gave him about two-thirds of his salary right through the War.

> When I finished at Wormwood Scrubs, I went before a Tribunal again. They accepted I was honest and I got my ticket, on condition I did land work or hospital work...they dressed me in civvies and gave me my fare home.

I applied to several hospitals in Edinburgh and they wouldn't have me because I was a 'conshie'... However, strolling in Colinton, a suburb of Edinburgh, I passed a nursery garden and went in and asked if the owner could give me a job. And he said, 'Delighted. Can you dig?'...So I worked for him for a couple of years, often in the nursery itself, but often in private gardens round about...Colinton is a community of pretty douce Edinburgh bourgeoisy people, where you would have expected them to look down their noses at 'conshies', but they didn't.

I didn't know a dandelion from a daisy when I started but I got books out of the library, of course, and swotted them up and became, I think, a pretty good jobbing gardener. On one occasion a professional jobbing gardener, who had been at it all his life, and myself dug over a lady's garden and when we finished he looked at it and said, 'That's the way I like to see it. None o' thae bloody flowers.' I was perfectly happy. Growing plants and flowers in the nursery I got 1s. 6d. an hour—the boss got 2s. 6d. an hour.[10]

MacCaig's second child, Ewen, was born while he was a gardener. After the War, MacCaig returned to teaching.

He wrote several poems over the years in an anti-War and anti-political mood. As stated earlier, he had an immense distrust of politicians. His poem 'Smuggler' sums up this distrust of the over-powering political 'giant'. It could refer to a political leader of any century, with his fine-sounding words but perhaps more suspect motives. Continuing the idea, he then went on in 'Leader of Men' to ridicule the politician whose 'nobility of vision' so affects him that his sight becomes blurred. This poem might refer to some of the political demagogues like Hitler, Mussolini, Stalin, men able to sway the masses by their rhetoric.

Sorley MacLean, the Gaelic poet, first met MacCaig in Sydney Goodsir Smith's house towards the end of the War. He had at that time a strong dislike of MacCaig's poetry which he felt was overburdened with imagery. However, when MacCaig published *Riding Lights* in 1955, MacLean began to admire his work, saying of his poetry:

It is wonderfully fertile in imagery. Quite a lot of modern English poetry is cluttered with images which you feel are not significant. What I like in MacCaig's poetry is its originality. Some people accuse him of being too clever, too witty and in a way too emotionally reticent altogether but there are certain things that really shake the heart.[11]

4. | In Lochinver

After the War, MacCaig returned to teaching at Craiglockhart Primary School. Early on in their married life, he and Isabel started to go up to the Lochinver area in Assynt for their annual holidays. Assynt (in Sutherland), which is on the coast that lies opposite Lewis, attracted them with its remoteness and its dramatic scenery. Also Isabel's family, on her father's side, came from Sutherland and, on her mother's side, from Caithness.

MacCaig had a 'love affair' with this land and sickened for it when he was away in 'stony' Edinburgh.[1] The area was to become a rich storehouse of images in his mind. He fattened up on these images during the summer and then later drew on this store to produce poetry when he was back in the city.

Most visitors to Lochinver travel north through the fishing port of Ullapool. As one then continues towards Lochinver, one can either take the main route or the slow, twisty, narrow scenic road, signposted to Achiltibuie. Travelling by this scenic road, one goes along the shores of Loch Lurgainn where Cul Beg hunches his huge shoulders above the road and further on one sees the crusty summit of Stac Pollaidh (Stac Polly). Small slices of red-gold sand glow along the loch side, islands dot the water and here and there lies a glassy pool at the edge of the loch, almost enclosed by land, where the water is very smooth and a pattern of grasses softens the dark green of the water. On a stormy day of mist and rain the main loch becomes choppy and the wind sings eerily in the telephone wires heightening the effects of remoteness and strangeness of this landscape. The mountains take on a grey and louring look, the mist rising from them like steam. Stac Pollaidh has a very dramatic look about it in this light with its craggy summit of sharp spires like the spine of a dinosaur. On the side of Loch Lurgainn one finds an odd little bird called the stonechat which looks rather like a plump sparrow. It sits on the telephone wires making a 'chat chat' noise at intruders into its territory:

> A flint-on-flint ticking—and there he is,
> Trim and dandy—in square miles of bracken
> And bogs and boulders a tiny work of art,
> Bright as an illumination on a monkish parchment.[2]

At the end of Loch Bad a Ghaill one takes the right fork in the road to Lochinver instead of driving on to Achiltibuie. From here one can see the other side of Stac Pollaidh, the bony head of Cul Mor and finally the ghost-like, thumb-shaped summit of Suilven. The scenery here is almost surreal with its strange series of sandstone mountains looming up suddenly from the lower ground like enormous reclining figures.

> Suilven and Cul Mor, my
> mountains of mountains,
> looming and pachydermatous in the thin light
> of a clear half moon.[3]

Approaching Lochinver, one passes Badnaban and Strathan. Seals, porpoises, basking sharks and even whales have been known to come in near the shore here. The local people are fishermen for white fish, lobsters and prawns. Lochinver and the surrounding small crofting communities are very remote from the rest of mainland Scotland. The other small centres of population are Stoer, Inverkirkaig, Badnaban, Clashnessie, Drumbeg and Inchnadamph. Lochinver is the main centre for all of these.

The MacCaigs spent some thirty summers in a cottage at Achmelvich, on the coast some miles north of Lochinver. The front door faces away from the sea and towards the land, presumably for shelter. When they stayed there the small fenced garden was semi-wild, full of nodding and bouncing varieties of wild flowers and long lush green grass. It was entered by a small wooden gate. There used to be a space under the door and a toad sometimes crawled in in the evenings to visit them and sit in the lobby.[4] The cottage was virtually unchanged from former times and it stood empty for most of the year except when the MacCaigs lived there. The main room was a dark room with a box bed and an open fire. There was a second room and there was also a bed in the attic. The byre end of the cottage, where cattle were kept in previous times, was sometimes used to house extra visitors.

When they first started to go to Achmelvich, the roads were very quiet and MacCaig used to cycle around a lot, particularly on the road which leads out to the lighthouse at Stoer Point, journeying along a very exposed piece of coastline where the North Sea stretches west as far as the eye can see. Looking south from this road, one sees the fringe of mountains—Suilven, Cul Mor, Cul Beg and Stac Pollaidh—so often referred to in the poems. In an evening sunset when the sandstone summits of these mountains turn pink and glow, this whole area acquires a strange magical quality.

From the road high above Stoer village, and looking south, can be seen a curious geological phenomenon on the coastline, called the Split Rock. The cluster of houses near it is called Clachtoll, which means in Gaelic 'the stone with the hole'. To get to the rock one has to walk round the bay and out over an area of rough and rolling grassland. In the spring and summer this area is full of wild flowers, and it was a place which recurred in MacCaig's memory frequently when he was home again.[5]

The cottage in which the MacCaigs stayed at Achmelvich
(photo: Marjory McNeill)

The huge Split Rock is so called because it has cracked in two, one part having moved several feet away out into the sea. Cormorants stand guard at the far side where the rock does a nose dive into the sea, and watch closely the mere human visiting the area. On a windy, dull day, the general effect of the towering rocks, the crevasse, the ever-moving turmoil of sea and the watching birds is very eerie.

> Long islands at their cables ride
> The double talk of the split tide
>> And a low black rock pokes out
>> From caves of green its dripping snout.[6]

Milne's Bar and Friendship
5. with Hugh MacDiarmid

I was standan at the bar, a glass in my nieve
Fleean wi the insolence of Friday nicht—
A rabble o' cronies, lauchter,
Blethers, din, the clink of glass,
The reik, the stour, the stink,
The blissit libertie of booze in action...
And there she was.[1]

In the late 1940s and throughout the 1950s, the literary scene in Edinburgh went through a particularly fruitful period. Several poets and writers, who were later to become famous, met up in Edinburgh in those years and frequented several Edinburgh pubs. As the writer Stanley Roger Green put it, writing of the 1950s, 'You couldn't have swung a claymore in the pubs of Milne's, Sandy Bell's or the Abbotsford without decapitating half a dozen aspiring or confirmed geniuses.'[2]

MacCaig first met Chris Grieve (Hugh MacDiarmid) in the Southern Bar in South Clerk Street in 1946. Also in the company that evening were Sydney Goodsir Smith and Sorley MacLean. MacCaig, later, talking to Roderick Watson in an interview on radio, told him:

And for a while they despised and rejected me, of course, because I write in English. 'Lickspittle of the English ascendancy; stabber in the back of the Scottish movement; cultural Quisling.' But of course, when they got to know me and found that I was tall, handsome, rich and could sing in tune, they decided I wasn't so bad after all and Douglas Young invented a phrase, he said 'It's a pity Norman doesn't write in Scots but he's got a Scots accent of the mind.' Whatever that means.[3]

During the Second World War MacDiarmid had worked in a Clydeside factory and on sea-going vessels based on the Clyde. After the War he became a reporter on the *Carlisle Journal*.

MacCaig and he were to become very close friends over the years. MacCaig said that while MacDiarmid did not influence him directly, he did so indirectly; that

MacDiarmid modified and qualified the way he responded to things. Asked by Roderick Watson whether there was a filial relationship between them, MacCaig replied, quietly and thoughtfully,

'Yes, in a way he was my son'![4]

Milne's Bar became their regular 'howff' or drinking place. In the late 1940s it was owned by a family called Lamont and had scrubbed tables and sawdust on the floor. In this time of immediate post-War shortages, Willie Lamont, who ran it, could get his customers twenty Capstan cigarettes when no one else could. Meetings there were at their best in the mid 1950s. The writers used to sit in a small back section of the bar which was a little room with one table and seats round the walls. At one time it had a door but this later disappeared. They got this section to themselves and here they held forth to one another on politics, religion, science, the arts, everything.

In Alasdair Gray's novel *1982 Janine* the narrator, Jock McLeish, describes the poets in the bar:

The bar was crowded except where three men stood in a small open space created by the attention of the other customers. One had a sombre pouchy face and upstanding hair which seemed too like thistledown to be natural, one looked like a tall sarcastic lizard, one like a small shy bear. 'Our three best since Burns,' a bystander informed me, 'barring Sorley, of course'.[5]

The three were, of course, MacDiarmid, MacCaig and Goodsir Smith. Another poet who often joined them in Milne's Bar was Tom Scott, noted for his red hair, his voluminous duffle coat and his attacking style in debate.

On one occasion an American doing research on the Scottish literati came all the way over the Atlantic just to meet them. He went to Milne's Bar and was shown into this corner and joined them for a drink. It was at the time that polyester shirts were becoming very popular. MacDiarmid and Sydney Goodsir Smith were discussing polyester shirts and carried on talking about them for two hours!

The poets always met in Milne's Bar informally. It was never arranged. MacCaig maintained that the Scots *hate* group activities and being herded into clubs. He related once a story about the futile attempt by some highly-educated Scots to form themselves into a group called the 'Makars' Club':

A number of fellows writing in Scots, recognising that they were spelling the thing differently, came to the conclusion that this was absurd, so they decided to establish an orthography, a way of spelling Scots that they would all use.

Their first meeting (about 1948-9) was in the Abbotsford Bar—a tiny back room—before Milne's day—and by some coincidence I happened to be there at the time so I joined them. About eight or ten people. They called themselves the Makars' Club. MacDiarmid could not be there at this first meeting but was immediately elected President and Douglas Young was elected Chairman. They then began to talk idly of this and that. Some said that Scots was dying in Burns' day. Others said, 'It is not dying at all, it is just that the intellectuals have forgotten their Scots—the common man has plenty Scots.' They discussed how to spell the present participle of something. Douglas was in the chair; a marvellous man, witty, learned—he had taught Greek in Aberdeen and Classics in St. Andrew's—and in the course of their strenuous studies came Douglas's turn to buy a round of drinks. The common wee working class man stuck his head in the door. Douglas said, 'Some more' (pronouncing it 'sum mair'). The wee fellow squeezed past and opened a window!

The next meeting of the Club was in Glasgow. They had this one other meeting and then it broke up. The Scots will not join things. They are very stubbornly independent. They could not even co-operate at the battle of Culloden. Half the other side were Scots. They think agreement is folly.[6]

However the poets of Milne's Bar did become well known and the bar was often referred to as 'The Poet's Pub'. The bar manager about this time was one Bob Watt. Alan Bold:

Abraham Adams, in *Another Little Drink* (1975) describes his alcoholic odyssey towards Milne's where Bob Watt waited like an unlikely Penelope and there was always a chorus of bards. Adams invokes Milne's, accurately, as 'a pub of character, presided over by the genial "mine host", Bob Watt...Lunchtime sessions in Milne's Bar became regular recurrences, and since I did not need to be back at work at any specified hour, I often lingered until Bob Watt raised the hated cry of "The ba's burst" at 3 p.m.'

Bob Watt's humour was legendary and he would swap jokes with the likes of Goodsir Smith who often arrived early for his restorative shot of Angostura bitters. Bob always ended a joke with a flourish, lifting a dirty glass and plunging it into the sink as a signal for laughter.[7]

In a poem called 'Kynd Kittock's Land', Sydney Goodsir Smith has given us a sketch of the poets in Milne's Bar. Talking first about poets of the past, he goes on to say:

> ...But ithers rise to tak their places brawlie;
> Grieve and Garioch aye tuim their pints,
> Mackie wheezes, Scott aye propheseeses
> Frae his lofty riggin tree
> While lean MacCaig stauns snuffin the Western seas
> And Brown leads wi his Viking chin
> And winna be rebukit.

George Mackay Brown, the Orkney writer, who is the 'Brown' referred to above, regularly came to Milne's Bar at this time. In fact, it is thought that one or two people who frequented this bar later appeared as characters in his plays. He described his impressions of these days:

> I was a student at Edinburgh in the late fifties, and soon found my steps tending in the direction of the pubs in Rose Street. There I looked, through the smoke and the beer-fumes, at the semi-legendary figures of Sydney Goodsir Smith, Norman MacCaig, Tom Scott, and (occasionally) Hugh MacDiarmid. I had read their poetry but did not have the courage to speak to them. At last they were kind enough to speak to me and invite me into their circle.
>
> There were two pubs between which the poets and artists moved, the Abbotsford and Milne's Bar. The Abbotsford is a handsome bar in a traditional Scottish style. About lunch-time there was a curious melling of business-men, B.B.C. people, and poets in the Abbotsford.
>
> Milne's Bar in those days was not a prepossessing place to look at. It had a large mirror with a swan on it that time was wearing away to a ghost—a kind of hexagonal 'snug', or telephone room—a room hidden round the back into which I penetrated only once—a large luncheon area with tatty tables and chairs. And yet it was an altogether delightful place to drink and talk in. I think the poets liked to be in Milne's more than anywhere. One of the attractions was that the staff were invariably pleasant and helpful; I think the manager, Bob Watt, set the tone of the place—he was an altogether delightful man, strict and accommodating at once, a true friend of the muses.
>
> The heroic laughter of Sydney Goodsir Smith could be heard in Milne's every day. I remember Norman MacCaig being there mostly on Friday and Saturday evenings. 'Quaich' he was called by Sydney and his other friends. His kind of humour was quieter and more subtle; if sometimes he took exception to a circumstance or a person his wit was quick as a rapier. To me he was invariably kind.[8]

At this time George Mackay Brown was not well known as a writer. He was a mature student studying English at Edinburgh University. Prior to this he had been at Newbattle Abbey, a residential adult education college near Dalkeith. The warden then was Edwin Muir, the poet and a fellow Orcadian, and Muir had a great influence on Mackay Brown, encouraging him, seeing the qualities he had. Mackay Brown said of this time:

> At Newbattle I had begun writing—poems mainly, purely for my own entertainment, like word games or crossword puzzles, although slightly better than that! From time to time I showed a few poems to Edwin Muir. Unbeknown to me, he sent them off to Hogarth Press and the next thing was a letter saying they wanted to publish them.[9]

If people were talking in Milne's Bar, Mackay Brown was quite content to listen. The conversations of the other writers were often sharp stuff and slagging each other. Whereas drink makes some people maudlin, with MacCaig it had the effect of

The
200 BURNS CLUB

Bards

HUGH MACDIARMID
NORMAN McCAIG
SYDNEY GOODSIR SMITH

Sydney Goodsir Smith, Christopher Grieve (Hugh MacDiarmid) and Norman MacCaig at the first 200 Burns Club supper, 20 January 1959
(photo: Scotsman Publications Ltd.)

loosening his tongue. A colleague said of him, 'If people drink like that and talk like that, I am all for drink. The words flow out. In that way he was a traditional poet.' Alan Bold:

It was not only Scottish poets who came to Milne's. I remember seeing Stevie Smith there, and W. H. Auden in his slippers and his cups. Both were in town for the Poetry International event. It was well known that Dylan Thomas had been in Milne's during his visit to Edinburgh in 1948. Around 1964 I spent an evening in Milne's with the Indian poet Dom Moraes and it was in the 'Poet's Pub' that I met Eileen O'Casey, the vivacious widow of the great Irish dramatist. It was said that you couldn't spill a pint in Milne's without putting a damper on some literary figure.[10]

After the sessions in Milne's were over, the poets, not satisfied with what they had so far said to one another, and wishing to continue, would leave at closing time and go on to someone's house, frequently MacCaig's. George Mackay Brown recalled:

In his own house he was a generous host; in this he had a good partner in Isabel, his wife. By 10 p.m., closing time in those days, the burn of lyricism and laughter was only beginning to gather head. Often a group of merry figures was to be seen at a bus-stop, burdened with 'cerry-oots', waiting for transport for Leamington Terrace.[11] Till well beyond midnight in Norman and Isabel's house, the burn poured on as merry-musical-dappled as Hopkins' Inversnaid or MacDiarmid's song of the waters in tumult. (Sometimes the great bard was there himself.) And it happened twice or thrice that a few of us went home from Leamington to breakfast at Marchmont, tired in body but deeply refreshed in spirit, after those mighty night-long word-splurgings.[12]

Sean O'Casey visited MacCaig's flat on one occasion in company with MacDiarmid. MacDiarmid wrote:

The last time I saw him he had come to Edinburgh to see the production of one of his plays at the King's Theatre. I did my utmost to have his presence in Scotland duly honoured and approached the Saltire Society and the Scottish Centre of the P.E.N. Club, but neither would move in the matter. Finally a party of friends arranged to meet in Norman MacCaig's house and we entertained Sean and Eileen, his wife, there. Sean was very quiet and would not drink. After a while, however, Eileen gave him a signal, pre-arranged no doubt, and Sean had a glass of brandy. It was as if a blind had been rolled up to let the sunshine in. Sean was in great form and even sang us a song.[13]

MacDiarmid and MacCaig were noted talkers. They frequently talked for hours and hours in MacCaig's house after the rest of the house had gone to sleep. Several friends have recalled these sessions in which they would 'flyte' or argue about some topic with the tenacity of two terriers worrying at a bone, each refusing to give in. They could be critical of one another's poetry. For instance MacCaig said that MacDiarmid sometimes contradicted his own ideas within the same poem. MacDiarmid too could be critical in his turn. Dolina MacLennan, the Gaelic singer, has recalled sitting one night in MacCaig's home listening to them. They went on for hour after hour talking about poetry and growing increasingly argumentative and insulting each other in a good humoured way. At last, as it was getting late, MacDiarmid attempted to draw things to a close and delivered his *coup de grâce*: 'After I am gone my poetry will be remembered and read for hundreds of years, but after you have gone, your poetry will soon be forgotten.'

MacCaig, ever aware of the older man's great fame, countered with, 'Ah, but *I* am not planning to go!'

But their love of arguing did not detract from the strong bond of friendship between them. MacDiarmid described in *The Company I've Kept* how MacCaig and he seemed to spark off ideas in one another by their long talks:

> ...the Scots when they are good talkers are the best talkers in the world. With F. G. Scott, Neil Gunn the novelist, and Norman MacCaig, the poet, in particular, all of whom have a Russian-like capacity for long-sustained talking, not at random but to a purpose—a thorough threshing out of ideas—I have many a time talked from supper one night till breakfast the next morning—ten or twelve solid hours of it—and these spates have released a lot of our best work. (As Logan points out in *The Scottish Gael* the pre-Union Scots like the Russians were great talkers and all-night 'cracks' were nothing out of the common. The later reputation of the Scots for being dour, taciturn, and limited in conversation to a few ayes, ums, and imphms is purely a post-Union product, as is the loss of the old gaiety and abandon and the development in lieu thereof of the appalling modern dullness and social gaucherie.)[14]

Another popular 'howff' in those days, much frequented by the poets, was the Abbotsford Bar in Rose Street. The atmosphere here was a trifle more 'up-market' than in Milne's. It is a most attractive relic of the Victorian era, with its ornamental central 'island' bar, and its partitioned seating. MacDiarmid used to meet people in the Abbotsford when he wanted to talk business.

George Mackay Brown noticed that beneath all the talking, laughing and joking that went on there was a sense of dedication in MacCaig, a quiet underlying sense of purpose:

> One was aware always that, for this particular man, poetry was the thing that mattered most (however recklessly we squandered words in Milne's or the Abbotsford or Leamington.) Subtle, invisible, passionate, the words that mattered were being gathered in the loom of his imagination; becoming at last, in the loneliness such as he must live in for much of the time, the magical web we call poetry.[15]

In 1955, MacCaig had a third book of poems published—*Riding Lights*. Reviewing the book, MacDiarmid wrote:

...we have been adjured to develop a distinctive Scots-English as Yeats developed a distinctive Irish-English. It is MacCaig's distinction that he has achieved just this. Yeats himself only achieved it in his later years. There is no Celtic Twilight about MacCaig's work; it is in the sunshine of the Gaelic classical tradition. (In other words, it realises what I meant when I said a quarter of a century ago that if there was to be a Scottish Literary Movement it must begin at the point where the Irish Literary Movement ended. Wherefore I can say to defeatists today: 'What? Retreat? Hell! We've only just got here.' MacCaig in fact is one of the very few who have 'got here'—and the only one who has done so through the medium of English.)[16]

The publication of *Riding Lights* followed a gap of nine years since *The Inward Eye* (1946). It showed a remarkable break away from the poetry of the forties into a far more lucid and communicative style. Here we see the emergence of the MacCaig that Louis MacNeice called 'a physical metaphysical'. In 'Summer farm', for instance, MacCaig seems to leave the morass of Apocalyptic images for the solid high-road of reality. The poet is lying in the grass—'not thinking'—and idly looking on a country scene and noting various beautiful images. Finally he does a backward somersault into himself and sees himself summer after summer on this spot:

> Self under self, a pile of selves I stand
> Threaded on time...

Riding Lights was a Poetry Book Society recommendation for 1955.

The next book of poems, *The Sinai Sort*, was published in 1957. Sydney Goodsir Smith wrote a review of this. A close friend of MacCaig, he started the article in a vein of robust humour, comparing MacCaig to Moses vaticinating from a cloud atop Mount Sinai. Goodsir Smith then went on:

The rather baffling title comes from a poem called 'The Golden Calf' in the course of which Mr MacCaig says

> The Moses in me
> Looks with a stone face on our gaudy lives

But the Moses in him is only one part of this poet, the school-teacher part; he is inclined to lecture the bewildered children, who are all those who cannot pick up his meaning at first throw.

The other part of him, the music-maker part, looks on life with the eyes more of a calf than a stone face, and gives us those many poems of landscape that are so immediately attractive.

There are fewer of these than there were in *Riding Lights* but they are as vivid and sensuous, yes magical, as ever. MacCaig is a master of landscape writing. In this kind of poem he uses words more as blobs of paint than notes of music; and yet the effect is musical, and always pungently atmospheric.

Here is a verse from 'November Night, Edinburgh':

> The night tinkles like ice in glasses.
> Leaves are glued to the pavement with frost.
> The brown air fumes at the shop windows,
> Tries the doors, and sidles past.
>
> I gulp down winter raw...

And here, as contrast, the first two verses from 'Clachtoll':

> Ships full of birds, like sailing trees,
> Add to the discourse of these seas
>   Whose flouncing skerries wash and sigh
>   A distance nearer with their cry.
>
> Long islands at their cables ride
> The double talk of the split tide
>   And a low black rock pokes out
>   From caves of green its dripping snout.

These are his most immediate poems and truly beautiful; he probably despises them himself and prefers his more thoughtful work where his danger is over-subtlety and obscurity.

He seems to use this obscurity as a shield between what the poem means to himself and what the reader can be allowed to get; it seems to be defensive as if, in a way, he was afraid or half-afraid he might be completely understood and the terrible secret be out.

That no power is lost with lucidity, but rather the opposite, is evident throughout the book in such poems (and they are the best of the book) as 'Another Flood', 'Shadow of Love' [*SS*, not in *CP*], 'Levels' [*SS*, not in *CP*], 'Sad Cunning', 'Brother'.

...I like him best when he is most direct and least obscure. I don't think this is just laziness for I find these poems stronger, more imperishable than his favourite subtleties of language and feeling. Get this book. MacCaig is a true bard—and there are not many about these days. There never were.[17]

Sydney Goodsir Smith came from New Zealand. His father was the famous Professor of Forensic Medicine at Edinburgh University, Sir Sydney Smith. Goodsir Smith at first studied medicine but abandoned it because he could not stand the anatomy classes—cutting up corpses. He then went to Oxford and did a degree in history. Returning to Edinburgh, he pursued a literary career as art critic, poet, dramatist, essayist and translator. He was also a gifted painter. He was particularly noted for his warmth of personality and his tremendous sense of humour. Stanley Roger Green called him a 'Rumbustious Falstaffian'. He became a close friend of both MacDiarmid and MacCaig. He loved to give his friends nicknames and, for instance, called Robert Garioch 'Beerioch'.

MacCaig was also a friend of the poet Edwin Muir. In April 1958, Muir, now an elderly man, wrote to MacCaig:

> I keep seeing poems by you everywhere, with friendly envy (if there is such a thing: I hope there is). How lovely to have the spring flowing freely...and not monotonously either, but with more variety than ever.[18]

In 1959 there appeared an anthology of poetry called *Honour'd Shade*.[19] It was edited by MacCaig and sponsored by the Arts Council of Great Britain. This anthology, which printed poems not previously printed in book form, introduced its readers to the work of several younger poets, including George Mackay Brown, Donald Macaulay, Edwin Morgan, Alexander Scott, Burns Singer, Iain Crichton Smith, Derick Thomson and Sydney Tremayne.

6. In Edinburgh

MacCaig was an Edinburgh man born and bred and loved living there. He and Isabel lived for many years in a first floor tenement flat in Leamington Terrace, which lies in a residential area of old established flats and terraced villas near the centre of the town, and where their son and daughter, Ewen and Joan, were brought up. After Isabel's death in 1990 until his own death he continued to live in this flat.

After the arrival of the two children, Isabel, although devoted to looking after her family, continued to teach, sometimes part-time, for quite a lot of their childhood. After this she started working for Oxford University Press and became one of the editors of the *Oxford Dictionary of Idiomatic English*.

One of MacCaig's sisters, Frances, lived in Edinburgh too and was an attractive, witty person, very interested in the arts. He was particularly close to Frances, who was the youngest sister and nearest to him in age. He wrote several poems about her, including 'Sounds of the day'. He had had a minor tiff with her and she had flounced out of the house in a temper. He took this contretemps and built on it to produce a very sad poem about the departure of a loved one—an example of how MacCaig uses one experience and builds and elaborates on it until it takes on a much larger significance.

In later life, MacCaig's parents lived in a house in Howard Place. His father, even after he retired, continued helping out in the shop until he was in his seventies. Although his father showed little apparent interest in his poems, MacCaig later discovered, after he had died, that he had in fact cut out and kept a lot of reviews of MacCaig's poetry from magazines and papers. There is something very 'Scottish' about this; the Scots as a race tend not to be excessive in their praise of anybody, particularly close relatives!

One year at Christmas, MacCaig visited his parents at Howard Place. His mother gave him some whisky. He drank a few sips and exclaimed at the tremendous potency and 'kick' it had. She told him that she had added a little surgical spirit to it! After his father's death, MacCaig's mother moved to a flat in Marchmont. Latterly one of her favourite pastimes, at which she excelled, was playing bridge. She died when she was over eighty.

Until he was in his late fifties, MacCaig taught in various schools in Edinburgh, including Craiglockhart and Parson's Green. By temperament a genial and happy person, he was a very good class teacher and got on with children. He used to get his pupils to produce some striking drawings and paintings. He had a technique for releasing their imaginations. He would say, 'Draw me a tree. Not green.' Once they embarked on that freedom they used to produce the most extraordinary things. One Christmas the children were illustrating the Flight into Egypt. One picture showed Joseph leading the donkey. The child's innocent eye and MacCaig's teaching methods had ended with the child producing a picture which had an almost surrealistic look about it.

He was a very tidy person. When he was a teacher, colleagues used to come into his room and be amazed at his desk. It had nothing on it! Their own desks would be laden with papers, books, etc. His writing is neat and small and the poems in style precise and trim. They are well-finished, tidy, craftsmanlike—almost like a piece of furniture. He once in fact compared the pleasure he got from writing poetry to the pleasure a carpenter might get from making a chair.

For a number of years, from about 1958 until 1967, he taught at Parson's Green Primary School, where he was Deputy Head. The original school backed on to the north east slopes of Arthur's Seat, high up above Piershill. MacCaig used occasionally in his lunch hour to go for a walk on Arthur's Seat. Children would go with him—strings of them—as if with the Pied Piper.

As Deputy Head he always taught the Primary 6 and 7 classes and he kept the children under control by a mixture of eloquence and sarcasm. Sometimes he sang to the children while teaching—little snatches of song to illustrate a point. The children and teacher in the room alongside used to stop working to listen to the songs which he sang in a sharp, edgy voice.

But there was always the pull of the other side of his life. He liked to keep his teaching activities within strict limits and was, for instance, never a very keen participant in extra-curricular activities. Obliged occasionally to referee football on a Saturday morning, he apparently looked totally out of place on the football field. He would stand in the middle of the field with a whistle. He never blew it and he never moved. He took it that the boys would know if they got a goal! He could never understand the offside rule.

Although MacCaig enjoyed teaching, he said himself that he 'hated children after half past three' and William Montgomerie, a friend, has recalled that: 'Norman picked up his fiddle as soon as he got home from school.'

MacCaig was turned down for a headmastership on several occasions during his teaching career because of being a 'conshie' (conscientious objector) during the War. He found this out when he met someone much later on who had been on some of the interview boards. He did in fact become a headmaster at the Inch School, Liberton,[1] for one year between working at Edinburgh and Stirling Universities. Hugh MacDiarmid, writing about MacCaig in *The Company I've Kept*, said, with typical MacDiarmid force:

Norman is a school teacher and one with a real vocation. He is now a deputy headmaster, but he ought to have been a headmaster long ago—and would have been if it had not been for the fact that he was a conscientious objector and served a term of imprisonment on that account. Every time for years the list of names for headmasterships was put forward, an ecclesiastical member of the Education Authority put a spoke in Norman's wheel on that account with that particular and unrelenting viciousness characteristic of many clergymen in relation to public affairs.[2]

All the time, as he moved around Edinburgh, MacCaig's ever-watchful eye was drawing in and storing images of the streets, buildings, odd occurrences, which were then subjected to his powerful ability to conjure with words. For instance, one day, driving in the centre of the town, he was halted by a policeman controlling traffic:

> The policeman stands on a plate of dirty light—
> Statue of liberty, angel with flaming sword
> As the whim takes him...[3]

He absorbed Edinburgh into his bones. He loved the city, its hills, its dirty depressing caverns between soaring tenements, its sleazy back streets, its proud Botanic Gardens, its Water of Leith, 'Puddocky',[4] the canal, the Grassmarket, Tollcross, Polwarth, the Grange—all are mentioned in poems. He wore Edinburgh like an old cloak, shrugged it on his shoulders. Edinburgh meant home and family to him.

He used to relish walking about the city after dark, particularly in the area of the High Street. Here he would pass through the old closes and up and down the worn staircases. If he had had a dram or two to drink, this heightened his perceptions and his awareness of the atmosphere of antiquity and decay.

His poems catch the sense of 'otherness' that descends on any city after dark when corners can acquire thick and threatening shadows and moonlight plays tricks on familiar stairs.

He appears in his poems to be 'triggered off' more by poverty than by wealth. Walking about the High Street and its closes in, say, the late fifties, he would be in the company of much poverty, of rotting buildings and—behind them—slums. Now many these have been renovated. Even today there are, however, still areas near the centre of Edinburgh where tall, gaunt buildings tower over dank closes and backyards and where the scent of decay lingers.

In some poems he recaptures very fleetingly images of Edinburgh's history. There is a series of curious poems conjuring up 'shadows of the past', e.g. 'Old Edinburgh' and 'Edinburgh Spring'. He also noted odd characters, tramps, vacant-eyed ladies with dilapidated prams, raucous street preachers breathing Hell and Damnation. MacCaig was sympathetic to these underdogs, the people whom polite society eyes askance.

The Grassmarket itself was, until the 1970s, a very downtrodden area, with its hideous Castle Trades Hotel, the only home of many down and outs who decanted themselves into the street during the day. MacCaig gives us glimpses of this 'other' side of Edinburgh in some of his poems.

MacCaig's Edinburgh: above, the Union Canal near his home in Leamington Terrace (photo: Seán Costello); *below, the Grassmarket in the Old Town* (photo: Michael McNeill)

In more jocular mood, in 'Gone are the Days', pretending to be a knight in shining armour, he achieves humour by juxtaposing the chivalry of the knight of old, visiting his lady love in her tower, with the fact that nowadays the 'knight' would buy his armour in Marks and Spencer's and his lady would lodge in a B & B establishment. He goes on to point out that, despite the modernisation of the myth, there are still wild places to be found in Edinburgh,

> ...There are wildernesses
> enough in Rose Street or the Grassmarket
> where dragons' breaths are methylated
> and social workers trap the unwary.

He ends by emphasising that love and romance have not died in the human heart, when he offers to buy his lady a love potion—'A gin, a double'! This is a poem that MacCaig used to read frequently at poetry readings and he always ended these last two lines by saying 'a gin, a double' with a rising intonation on 'double' to make it a question, the word taking on not just the sense of repetition of her order but also of astonishment at her brashness at ordering anything so powerful and expensive. There is a tiny sense of the Presbyterian Scotsman here!

'Nude in a fountain' (1960) is one of his early 'Edinburgh' poems. There are echoes of John Donne here—it is a complex, wordy poem full of fleeting images. Also at this time he published 'Edinburgh courtyard in July', arguably a much better poem, where he is using his artist's eye to paint a picture in words. He gets away from the stream of images and concentrates more on one spot and a few images. In its roughness and intensity this is like a work of Van Gogh; the light is smeared on the tenements, the buildings lean energetically into the light and hoist themselves aloft, 'cliff-dwellers' live in them, hanging out their 'brilliant rags' or washing. A whole thesis could be written on the similarities between certain MacCaig poems and the work of certain artists! His Edinburgh is no carefully shored up and preserved one where the local Council or some Arts Society have cleaned, restored, and redecorated. Not for him the polished delights of the museum-like tourist attractions. In 'Edinburgh Courtyard in July' he writes:

> Hot light is smeared as thick as paint
> On these ramshackle tenements. Stones smell
> Of dust. Their hoisting into quaint
> Crowsteps, corbels, carved with fool and saint,
> Holds fathoms of heat, like water in a well.
>
> Cliff-dwellers have poked out from their
> High cave-mouths brilliant rags on drying lines;
> They hang still, dazzling in the glare,
> And lead the eye up, ledge by ledge, to where
> A chimney's tilted helmet winks and shines.

And water from a broken drain
Splashes a glassy hand out in the air
That breaks in an unbraiding rain
And falls still fraying, to become a stain
That spreads by footsteps, ghosting everywhere.

But he did not only confine himself to old Edinburgh. One of his favourite spots was the canal near his home, where he depicted the effect of the seasons on the still water and its plant and animal life in such poems as 'Spring in a clear October', 'Preening swan' and 'Canal in winter'.

In 'Spring in a clear October', like 'Nude in a fountain', we have a complex, lyrical piece of work. The poem is rather freer verse in that it has no rhymes, but the stanzas are metrically regular—formal to that extent. It is a beautiful poem but perhaps over-laden with images.

In 'Botanic Gardens' he sees the city's Botanic Gardens as a Garden of Eden guarded by a 'keeper with a hating face' who tries to stop the Edinburgh visitors from enjoying its delights. The keeper is forever lurking amongst the plants, casting his malevolent eye on people and when he sees a latter day Adam and Eve who have the temerity to kiss each other, they are then driven from the gardens by the keeper— 'a flaming by-law in his hand'. This poem is a protest against petty officialdom and the foolishness of man; about how people try to cramp one another, to confine one another by rules and regulations so that even the enjoyment of flowers becomes regulated by a clock-watching official. Here one finds two recurring themes of MacCaig—his love of nature and beauty and his dislike of those who try to confine and control other people.

Edinburgh is in many ways a curious place. It is not a city that people tire of quickly. It has many faces and many strata of society within it—some people would not recognise its other faces if they saw them, moving only in their own restricted areas and amongst other similar people. It is however, on the whole, a strongly 'middle class' city, a beautiful city, one to take a pride in. Robert Garioch wrote many tongue in cheek poems about it.[5]

MacCaig caught many of Edinburgh's faces in his work but he is not a descriptive poet, his poems reflect moods rather than places. His Edinburgh is distorted too. None of the pageantry, the richness, the 'show off' side of Edinburgh is seen in the poems. Very often he is at the centre of the poem, walking about. The poems are not about Edinburgh, they are about how Edinburgh and he relate to one another. For instance, MacCaig does not describe an Edinburgh antique shop, he observes himself and a lady in the window and writes a love poem ('Antique shop window') in which the shop contents and his and her reflections become intermixed.

Although he frequented the pubs of Rose Street and Hanover Street, he wrote few poems describing them or their customers, apart from 'Milne's Bar': and here the bar could be almost empty, for the whole poem concentrates on himself and a friend talking and MacCaig watching his own face in the mirror. The rough and tumble, the noise and variety of pub life, is not recorded—what interests MacCaig is analysing how he himself reacts to the rather boring friend telling him his problems. He is a very restrained and selective poet in this way. The final poem contains only the very refined essence of an event or an experience.

There is a poem about a lady pianist at a concert—'Concerto'—presumably set in Edinburgh. But here again, there is no description of the concert hall, nor of the lady. The poem concentrates in comic fashion on her rather poor technique and the polite audience who suffer her playing with fortitude!

In 1984 he won an award from the Society of Authors to travel abroad and meet other writers. He got leave of absence from Parson's Green School to travel to Italy just after Easter and went to Florence, Venice, Rome and Verona. However, he got tired of the tourist spots and so he went off the beaten track a bit. In particular he visited L'Aquila.

Strangely, although he loved Italy, he wrote very few poems about it. 'Assisi' is perhaps one of the best known of these. It concerns a dwarf sitting outside the churches in Assisi which were built in honour of St Francis. First he points to the dwarf. Then he speaks of the Christian teachings of the priest and finally he describes the tourists fluttering along in the wake of the priest, ignoring the dwarf, who is begging for money. The poem, in an oblique way, criticises the tourist at religious shrines—so absorbed in the glories of the past that he does not see the needs of the present. Also it is a protest against injustice—all that wealth in the churches built for 'the brother of the poor' contrasted with the poor human beggar outside it.

Another of the few poems set in Italy is 'The streets of Florence'. In typical MacCaig style, we do not get a description of the city. No warm colours, no talkative Italians, no sunburn or ice cream. His poem is introspective and philosophical and speaks of the similarity in the faces of the modern Florentines walking in the street outside the art gallery to those on the walls within it; of how we cannot escape our roots; we are all linked to our ancestors, part of a continuous line of creation.

But MacCaig was a home bird. He was not a keen traveller and had no particular wish to explore the world. He once said that he would travel overseas once he had finished writing about what there was to write about here—'In other words, never!'

He had many poems printed over the years in the *Edinburgh Evening Dispatch*. The poems to be published were selected by the journalist and poet Albert Mackie. Lots of people sent in poetry to this paper. They used to throw out the 'duds' and put the rest into a drawer. When they had a bit of space left over in the paper they would hunt through the drawer for a poem to fit the space. Albert Mackie would say something like: 'I want one three inches long from the poetry drawer'!

Karl Miller, the writer, has recalled how, when he was still a pupil at the Royal High School, he met MacCaig one evening, by chance. (They had previously been introduced briefly at a meeting in Edinburgh.)

One night shortly afterwards I ran into him again in the vestibule of the General Post Office where we spent an hour talking about the imagery of Lorca. The GPO was the hub of the Edinburgh I have been describing, with its wild lives, its prim lives, the 'heavenly Hanoverianism'—in Burn's phrase—of its handsome squares and thoroughfares, and the loyal names that were prudently conferred on these by the magistrates who built the New Town: facing me across a street sloe-black in the rain was the Cafe Royal, to my left was Princes Street, and at my back was the Royal Mile. MacCaig did not seem to mind spending an hour talking about Lorca with a schoolboy he hardly knew (only Lorca, we said, could have provided that image of a bisected apple), and the encounter was typical of the town as I knew it then, of its grave interest in literature and of its private courtesy.[6]

Recurring Traits
7. in the Early Poetry

> A heron, folded round himself,
> Stands in the ebb, as I in mine,
> I feel my world beneath me, like his, shelving
> To darker depths of dark and bitter brine.[1]

In the books of poetry published from 1955-66 there appeared much work of a metaphysical nature. The books in question are *Riding Lights* (1955), *The Sinai Sort* (1957), *A Common Grace* (1960), *A Round of Applause* (1962), *Measures* (1965), and *Surroundings* (1966).

Riding Lights starts off with a poem called 'Instrument and agent' concerning the perception of the individual: how each person sees everything slightly differently from the next person because it is coloured by his own thoughts and imaginings and past experiences. This idea was to recur again and again in future poems.

> In my eye I've no apple; every object
> Enters in there with hands in pockets.
> I welcome them all, just as they are,
> Every one equal, none a stranger.
>
> Yet in the short journey they make
> To my skull's back, each takes a look
> From another, or a gesture, or
> A special way of saying *Sir*.
>
> So tree is partly girl; moon
> And wit slide through the sky together;
> And which is star—what's come a million
> Miles or gone those inches farther?

MacCaig's poems are often deceptive. One thinks one is reading a poem about a scene but it turns into a poem about a relationship. Most of his poems are in fact about people or animals or birds.

Another recurring theme in his poetry is that of the poet watching himself. The poem 'Same day' is one of the early 'Edinburgh' poems, and in it the poet is watching the dawn from the window of his flat (MacCaig was a person who needed very little sleep.) It is full of metaphysical ideas and metaphors, e.g.:

> Someone like me walks solitary in the street;
> His footsteps put a roof over the morning
> And a hollow under it.

He has shaken off his obscure Apocalyptic cloak and emerged into a world of odd perceptions and of intense self-awareness.

> And someone like me, here, with a pen for crutch,
> Limps out into the light, afraid to look back.
> Will I be here to welcome him again
> When other midnights strike?

In 'Waiting to notice' we find a very typical MacCaigian introspective poem. The poet is often trying to do the impossible and stand back and see his own mind at work. He is very much aware of how it is affected by where he is. In the wilds his mind unwinds, his intellect gets a rest and he waits for 'fancy' to take over. He is a fanciful poet—a poet of fantasy even. He sees one thing and 'sees' another through it. There is a touch of surrealism in this poem where a Dali-like image of the poet as a stone statue appears:

> I sprawl among seapinks—a statue
> fallen from the ruins
> of the air into
> the twentieth century...

Later in the poem he steps even further into surrealism. Noting how the sun shows dancing specks of dust not normally seen, he tries to imagine how it would be if by a shaft of light he could see the 'invisible dancing' of his own imagination. This also ties in with MacCaig's fascination with nature and its workings, his zest for life, his love of showing how rich and strange is the commonplace if one really looks and thinks about it.

Another recurring trait is his personification of animals and birds. This was particularly strong in his early and middle period poetry. In *A Common Grace* we find the comic poem 'Goat' in which he gives the goat all sorts of human and rather sinful qualities. Something of the feeling in this poem was later repeated in 'Leaving the Metropolitan Museum' in which he describes his thoughts on seeing Picasso's iron statue of a goat, only in the latter poem, instead of simply celebrating the characteristic qualities of the goat, he extolls Picasso's ability to capture the animal by his art.

Sometimes he puts himself into the poem as a God-figure with power over the animal world. In 'Feeding ducks' the ducks appear to him to 'worship' at his feet for the bread that he feeds them with. Similar imagery is found in 'World within world' (*MP*, not in *CP*).

Most of the poems at this time have a formal structure. They have a finished, tidy quality, although lines are grouped in units of varying length and the actual rhythms of the lines are seldom completely regular.

'Celtic cross' is particularly notable for its very complex structure. The rhyme is A B B C A C. The lines are roughly two long, two short and two long. As a result of this elaborate structure, it reads with a complex rhythm, having a pause in the centre of each stanza between the two short lines, and it seems in words to mirror the intricate interweaving of the patterns carved on the Celtic cross. The whole poem is full of images of intertwining carving, singing voices, serpents, and generations of people.

At this time, the effects of sunlight on objects fascinated him—in *A Common Grace* (1960) we look at sunlight on tenements, window ledges, on the water in the canal. 'World's centre' is a rather metaphysical poem about a petal on the inside of a window ledge and how the sunlight playing on it gives it a mathematical setting within the world scheme of things.

In 'Haycock, Achiltibuie', he looks at sunlight on hay. Here 'Van Gogh' MacCaig is at work. This is a very sensuous poem, full of references to touch, smell, taste and sound. He looks at a rather dilapidated haystack which is daily dwindling from the effects of the weather. The poem contains elements of his later very famous poem 'Byre' in its use of Biblical imagery—the haycock being many mansions 'where mice, its little sinners, can run in'.[2] In the former poem, a Van Gogh-type crofter appears and hoists the 'Zion' of the mice on his back and makes off with it.

'Jug' is reminiscent of one of the Impressionists. It celebrates an ugly little jug of flowers trying to elbow its way into importance. With a sudden dash of comic exuberance, MacCaig describes it as:

> This odd neurosis that explodes its joys
> Like a wild vice in the bosom of Mrs Grundy.

Here the metaphysical intellectual is diverted into humour, rare in the early poems—but the humour in MacCaig's poetry was to grow and develop over the years until it became almost the *raison d'être* for some poems.

MacCaig often said that one of the people who influenced him as a poet was John Donne. In Donne's poem, 'The Comparison' we have the piling up of sensuous images, the relish for the sounds of words that we find in MacCaig: Donne is here writing in an earthy, humorous and intellectual way all at the same time:

> As the sweet sweat of roses in a still,
> As that which from chafed musk cat's pores doth trill,
> As the almighty balm of th'early east,
> Such are the sweat drops on my mistress' breast

And on her neck her skin such lustre sets
They seem no sweat drops, but pearl carcanets.
Rank sweaty froth thy mistress' brow defiles,
Like spermatic issue of ripe menstrous boils
Or like that scum, which, by need's lawless law
Enforced, Sanserra's starved men did draw
From parboiled shoes, and boots...

M. H. Abrams says of Donne:

Donne set the metaphysical pattern by writing poems which are sharply opposed
to the rich mellifluousness, the sense of human dignity, and the idealized view of
sexual love, which had constituted a central tradition in Elizabethan poetry,
especially in the writings of Spenser and the Petrarchan sonneteers. Instead,
Donne wrote in a diction and meter modeled on the rough give-and-take of actual
speech, and usually organized his poems in the dramatic and rhetorical form of an
urgent or heated argument—with a reluctant mistress, or an intruding friend, or
God, or Death, or with himself. He employed a subtle and often deliberately
outrageous logic; he was realistic, ironic, and sometimes cynical in his treatment
of the complexity of human motives, especially in the sexual relation; and whether
playful or serious, and whether the poetry of love or of intense religious experience, he was persistently 'witty', making ingenious use of paradox, pun, and
startling parallels and distinctions.[3]

Mary Jane W. Scott, speaking of the influence of Donne on MacCaig, wrote:

Scottish tradition is certainly full of adaptations and imitations of classical literature, including the work of the unfortunately-termed Scottish Chaucerians and
the seventeenth Century Scots Metaphysicals; however, MacCaig has felt the
influence of the English Neoclassical tradition in poetry more directly than through
those imitative or derivative works in Scots. He readily admits great admiration
for the poetry of John Donne and says that Donne's poetry is one of the very few
'discernible' influences on his own work. Donne was, of course, in the line of
development from the Italian Renaissance, notably Dante, whose lucid imagery,
accurate diction and sure formal elegance he adopted. Like Dante and Donne,
MacCaig has developed the ability of saying difficult things with apparent sim-
plicity. He appreciates the compression and clarity possible within such strictly
formal verse, and shares with his models Dante and Donne a similar philosophical attitude to the world they see. MacCaig is a poet always aware of other sides
to reality, possibilities beyond the initially apparent visual world, and, with skilful
Metaphysical wit of extended inversion, he presents this realm of Platonic otherness
as an equally 'real' alternative. The comparisons of vastly different things within
Metaphysical conceits strengthen the tangible 'reality' of each object perceived.
Constant restraint of the poetic imagination is vital to this mode, and both Donne

and MacCaig are able to speculate on the complex nature of the universe, by working through strict form. Their imaginative and supremely intellectual inquiry and its poetical expression is thus very similar; indeed, the poetry is witty and deeply thought-provoking.[4]

Some of MacCaig's poems about women are written (Donne-like) in the first person with the poet addressing the woman. Others, which start off talking about landscape or some other inanimate object, turn into poems about a woman. The women in the early poems are almost always shadowy and insubstantial—one learns nothing about them, not even the colour of their hair.

In *Riding Lights* MacCaig wrote a very effective poem about the breaking up of a relationship called 'You went away', in which he speaks directly to the woman. It starts:

> Suddenly, in my world of you,
> You created time.
> I walked about in its bitter lanes
> Looking for whom I'd lost, afraid to go home.

There are similarities between this poem and Donne's 'The Apparition':

> When by thy scorn, O murderess, I am dead,
> And that thou think'st thee free
> From all solicitation from me,
> Then shall my ghost come to thy bed...

MacCaig's poem portrays the bitterness of loss and shows a hypersensitive side to his nature. There is a nightmare quality to the first two stanzas with the idea that one can 'possess' another and that the person 'possessed' can steal himself or herself back. As the poem continues, he describes how the hurt mind sees the physical world as 'rotting'. There is a vicious, violent tone to the last stanza, similar to the vicious violent tone of Donne's poem.

An occasional theme in the poems about women concerns the poet's almost psychic ability to conjure up the woman who is absent, to bring her back to his presence, if only in his mind. 'Poem for a goodbye' is an example of this. This time the poet has been separated by circumstances from the loved woman and says that distance cannot end their love—it will survive the effects of distance and the passage of time. Again it is written in the first person with the poet addressing the woman. Here again there are echoes of Donne, this time of his 'A Valediction: Forbidding Mourning':

> Our two souls therefore, which are one,
> Though I must go, endure not yet
> A breach, but an expansion,
> Like gold to aery thinness beat.

In 'Standing in my ideas' we have a lyrical poem in praise of a young woman. There is here a touch of Shakespearean imagery: he speaks of 'Nature, that vogue mistress'. It is a complex poem. The girl is totally obscured in a net of beautiful words.

MacCaig said that, in addition to Donne, he was also influenced by Wallace Stevens. The poetry of Stevens has a luscious, exotic quality about it. Like MacCaig's, his poems are often obscure and enigmatic. One gets a glimpse of a magnificent view—no explanation.

Stevens seems a very poetic poet: more in love with the way he says things than with what he is saying. He is weaving a spell, saying an incantation, conjuring up colours and shapes out of mere words on a page. His scenery—Florida and Key West—is more exotic than that of MacCaig. He has some marvellous and extraordinary statements to make. On the correlation between music and emotion he writes:

> Music is feeling then, not sound;
> And thus it is that what I feel,
> Here in this room, desiring you,
> Thinking of your blue-shadowed silk,
> Is music.[5]

Stevens' poems have been compared with the pictures of Rousseau. W. Y. Tindall states in *Seven Modern American Poets*:

Evading analysis, 'The Virgin Carrying a Lantern' is indefinitely suggestive. It is a picture—like something by Rousseau, *le douanier*. It is a strange experience, and its meaning, like that of a picture, is what it is. 'A poem', says Stevens in *Adagia*, 'need not have a meaning and like most things in nature often does not have'.[6]

Stevens was more of a hedonist in his poems than MacCaig. He loved and wrote about wine, pictures and roses. He in fact collected pictures. Tindall says of Stevens: 'Voyaging around his chamber was enough for this mental traveler, and his office an adequate asylum.'[7]

There are a few lines of Stevens' which one might say are exactly echoed in MacCaig's own philosophy:

> I was the world in which I walked, and what I saw
> Or heard or felt came not but from myself;
> And there I found myself more truly and more strange.[8]

Wallace Stevens' *Collected Poems* was published in 1955. He worked for the Hartford Accident and Indemnity Company. Like MacCaig he was an unassuming man, quietly devoted to the perfection of his own idiom.

MacCaig, talking about the subject matter of poetry, pointed out on one occasion that poetry can say very little and yet be great poetry. This was during an interview with Alastair Moffat in MacCaig's home. MacCaig here said:

> You use ideas to put words in a certain organised order—rhythm, sounds, ideas, metaphors, rhymes—in order to create a thing which we call a poem. It uses these things to create something that we call poetry. That is all. That is all. The ideas are nothing. Nothing! 'Full fathom five thy father lies.' O.K. He is drowned. What is a fathom—six feet? 'Of his bones are coral made.' Rubbish. 'These are pearls that are his eyes.' Balderdash! And then it goes on to some claptrap about sea nymphs ding dong belling—absolute rubbish! But it is a great poem. It has resisted the malice of time for three centuries and it is a clotted confection of nonsense.
>
> The only way you can tell a poem from a non-poem is the nature of the response. The poem might be written in prose. Outward form has got nothing to do with it. There are chunks in the Old Testament which are obviously poetry though they are written in prose form. It is the nature of the response that distinguishes poetry from other kinds of writing. Poetry may use ideas to make a poem but you don't go to poetry for ideas. 'Cover her face, mine eyes dazzle. She died young.' Is that not marvellous? What is the idea? 'Chuck a towel over the lassie's face.'
>
> The thing that influenced me in a way, in this very house, is MacDiarmid and two other fellows. The two other fellows mentioned Mr R. Burns, as Chris[9] liked to call him, and what do you think is Burns's greatest line of verse. One of them quoted, the other quoted and then they said to Chris, who for 40 years had been saying 'The poetry of ideas, the scientisation of poetry, the bridging of the cultures', you know, and they asked him what he thought was Burns's best line and I expected one from the so-called political poems or satirical poems and he said, 'The best line Burns ever wrote was 'Ye are na Mary Morison!' Now if I were to say to you 'Ye are na Mary Morison' you would agree, but you would not be impressed, but if you put these four words into the verse:
>
>> Yestreen, when to the trembling string
>> The dance gaed thro' the lighted ha',
>> To thee my fancy took its wing,
>> I sat, but neither heard or saw;
>> Tho' this was fair, and that was braw,
>> And yon the toast of a' the town,
>> I sigh'd and said amang them a',
>> 'Ye are na Mary Morison!'
>
> How can a man invest four ordinary words with such a weight? Amazing![10]

But MacCaig is nothing if not diverse. No sooner does one begin to feel that his poetry is falling into some category than he appears in another guise. Some rather unusual poems appeared in *A Round of Applause* (1962). 'Explorer' is, for instance, an early example of a 'character sketch' or 'tiny narrative' type of poem. It is an immensely rumbustious piece, full of swaggering energy, describing the bluff sailor who risks death and disaster to explore the world, 'Trampling new seas with filthy timbers...' He relies on the Bible and his courage to see him through:

> ...When sails were gone
> Bundling and tumbling down the shrieking dark,
> He trailed the Bible as sea-anchor; when
> Reefs shaved the barnacles from the keel, he took
> His gentlemanly snuff...

In the final stanza this larger-than-life adventurer falls asleep:

> He logged the latest, drank his grog and spread,
> With only one uncomprehending sigh,
> His wild uncharted world upon his bed.

In this sort of poem MacCaig is getting right away from the intellectual conjuring tricks of his early work—he is telling us a story, painting a picture. This poem could perhaps be compared with a later poem 'Mrs Grant' (1969) in its feeling of a character at odds with the world. It also has similarities to the description of a robust fisherman in 'Uncle Roderick'.

Another poem which is rather out of the ordinary appeared in *A Round Of Applause*. This is the cinematic 'Thaw on a building site'. Again there is a tremendous feeling of a lot of things all starting to happen at once, which MacCaig achieves by very selective, short, rapid phrases; and in the middle of the poem he places, as a sort of centrepiece:

> A concrete mixer cleared its throat
> For a boring speech, all consonants...

At the end of the poem is an image which reminds one of a film of a building collapse, put into reverse:

> ...And, slowly, buildings
> backed their way into the light;
> They crumbled upwards into being.

'Skittles' is also full of energy and movement, with a cinematic quality. It is an unusual poem—one of the 'one offs'. It is comic in that the poet, playing skittles, rolls the ball badly, and instead of making for its target it turns itself into a toad and hobbles along erratically. The poet, assuming defeat, stands up:

> From snake to mantis to man
> I stand upright and turn away...

49

8. Friends in Lochinver

The MacCaigs became regular visitors to Assynt, staying in the cottage at Achmelvich every summer. When they first started going up there, they got to know a good few people, but it was difficult for them to make close friends as the local people were reticent and retiring with strangers.

However, one day, after watching a rowing race, MacCaig got talking to one of the winning team, a certain Angus K. MacLeod, in the Culag Bar at Lochinver, and thus started a friendship which was to last until MacLeod died. Getting to know MacLeod (or 'A.K.', as he was called) and his wife, Kitty, was MacCaig's key to entry into Lochinver society, because MacLeod belonged there and knew everyone.

MacLeod was a spare, wiry man, bright-eyed and energetic. People and animals took to him readily. Within a few minutes of meeting a stranger, he could make that stranger feel completely at home. Children liked him instantly and climbed up on his knee. He and Kitty lived in a house in Inverkirkaig—some miles south of Lochinver, round the coast road.

MacCaig and MacLeod went fishing a great deal. Both could walk tirelessly for miles to get to the fishing grounds, in fact MacLeod was a very rapid walker. He seemed to have eyes all round his head and could see some tiny stags on the hill, for instance, long before anyone else would notice them. They fished in the innumerable lochs and rivers of Assynt. A convenient stand-by spot was the estuary very near MacLeod's house, from the Red Rock Pool down to the Sea Pool.

Some poaching goes on in the Sutherland area. In his day MacLeod relieved the hills and streams of a fair number of stags and salmon—but always for the pot. He was in fact hauled up several times for poaching but was very recalcitrant when ticked off, flatly refusing to stop his activities. In fact MacLeod's father, who had been a ghillie, was given a fearful row by the local landowner when he was caught (aged 84) trying to catch a salmon!

It is quite usual in this area for a man to work at perhaps two or even three part-time occupations at the same time. MacLeod ran a shop, looked after a bit of land, and acted as roadman. At one point, in order to make some extra money, he had a hut put up on a piece of his land. He and his wife lived in the hut in the summer and let their house to visitors—usually families staying for a month at a time. People were drawn to him by his friendliness and his hut was a popular place, sometimes overflowing with company:

> It clamps itself to a rock, like a limpet,
> And creeps up and down in a tide of people,
> Hardly ever stranded in a tideless sabbath:
> A pilgrimage place where all hymns are jubilant.[1]

MacLeod was a well read man with a quick mind and rapid wit. He also had built up a whole philosophy of his own based on his experiences working out on the hills or on the sea and rivers fishing. Like MacCaig he had a capacity for sustained talking and for arguing about matters ranging from the most trivial to the most profound.

He and MacCaig used to talk and talk, particularly in the evenings. The subjects ranged from philosophy to practical matters. Sometimes they would talk about fishing in the abstract or about the concept of the 'absolute'. MacLeod said there was no such thing—that it was a foolish construct. But the next moment they might be talking about what fly to use on such and such a river.

They used to argue like mad. MacCaig said of this: 'We both agreed that argument, especially when it rises to the heights of vituperation, is an art form to be indulged in for its own sake and whatever you are arguing about does not matter— They were not all about nothing!'[2]

For example, one night they visited a mutual friend at a house nearby and there were two pictures hanging on the wall. They discussed these. MacCaig said he preferred one and MacLeod said he preferred the other. They started arguing. Starting from that they branched out in several directions into the nature of art, the values of colours, the importance of shapes.

When they were sitting in A.K.'s hut of an evening, the long-suffering Mrs MacLeod (in the next room) would often hear them arguing through the plywood partition. In fact, they sometimes talked until it was daylight again. But eventually the argument would reach a certain stage and they would suddenly decide to abandon it. They would clap down their hands on the table and give up the wrangle. MacLeod would retire to bed and MacCaig would set off to walk home.

Generally he would refuse a lift, insisting on walking by himself. Presumably this explains why there are several poems written about night scenes in and around Achmelvich, Inveruplan, etc. MacCaig enjoyed these walks. He reckoned things looked very different at night. Generally he would have had a dram or two and his awareness was heightened by this. He saw ordinary things in a way that he wished he could see them every day or night.

In the poem, 'Loch Roe', he is out in the dark looking at moonlight on the sea loch near his cottage at Achmelvich. Here he plays with the idea of the loch and the hills being like a city square and tenements. The first stanza is full of images of stillness. In the second stanza two porpoises appear, patrol the loch like policemen, and leave. In the final stanza, stillness returns. Not only does he make these strange correspondences between wild places and cities, he then blends these parallel images into a poem.

The poem 'Walking to Inveruplan' describes a night walk. On this occasion he was making his way from Achmelvich to Inveruplan to visit Charlie Ross, the game-keeper, to attend one of the social gatherings which the Rosses sometimes held in their cottage. The person who was to give him a lift had failed to turn up so, carrying his bottle of whisky for the party, he had set out to walk. It was getting dark and the moon was rising. In the poem, he imagines that as he goes along he takes a nip or two of the 'hard stuff' to sustain him and this fires his imagination and he begins to feel that he has for once been invested with great wisdom about the meaning of life.

> Glowing with answers in the aromatic dark,
> I walk, so wise,
> Under the final problem of lit skies.
>
> I reach the bridge, where the road turns north to Stoer,
> And there perch me
> Under the final problem of a tree.
>
> I'm in a Li Po mood. I've half a mind
> To sit and drink
> Until the moon, that's just arisen, should sink.
>
> The whisky's good, it constellates. How wise
> Can a man be,
> I think, inside that final problem, me.
>
> If you are short of answers, I've got them all
> As clear as day...
> I blink at the moon and put the bottle away
>
> And then walk on (for there are miles to go
> And friends to meet)
> Above the final problem of my feet.

The 'aromatic dark' possibly refers to the scent of bog myrtle which has a strong balsam-like fragrance, particularly after rain, and which grows profusely on the west coast. Li Po was a philosopher and one of China's greatest poets. There is a very famous Chinese picture of him, 'Li Po By A River Drinking Madly By Moonlight'. In fact MacCaig's poem is a mixture of two separate experiences—walking to a ceilidh and drinking in the moonlight. For, as MacCaig later pointed out—'Do you think I would be drinking my whisky on the way there?'[3]

The ceilidhs at Charlie Ross's were known locally as 'horo-geallaidhes' (pronounced 'horoyallies'). Charlie Ross, a heavily built, strong man, was a close friend of the MacCaigs and of MacLeod. He was very fast on the intellectual draw and typically had a quick riposte. His wife would arrange the get-together by mentioning

A.K. Macleod (left) and MacCaig on the pier at Lochinver, about 1970

to people 'We will have an evening'. They were held at any time of year and usually on a Friday night. Although the house was small, it was beautifully warm. Everybody brought his statutory half bottle. Charlie Ross laid them flat on the sideboard because, as he said with awe, 'We had an accident once!'

Usually there would be about eight people present. They were local people and, very occasionally, visitors. They were mostly men and were all 'buddies'. They were given a huge meal by Mrs Ross and then they drank and sang and argued. The ceilidhs often went on till what MacCaig called 'pitch daylight'. Practically everybody had a particular song they sang. Bill Simpson, the actor, was at one or two of these. He was extremely good at reading in broad Scots, particularly Burns. These ceilidhs were also held in other houses in the area. The ceilidhs stirred up within their participants an extraordinary feeling of 'community' and closeness.

> But the night's not over. A twinkle of light
> in Strathan, Brackloch, Inveruplan, shows
> where the tales are going round, tall
> as the mast of the *Valhalla*, and songs are sung
> by keeper, shepherd and fisherman,
> each tilting his Rembrandt face in the light
> and banging the chorus round, till, with a shout
> he takes up his dram and drinks it down.
> *The Gauger of Dalmore* lives again
> in verses. An old song
> makes history alive again,
> as a rickle of stones peoples the dark theatre
> of the mind with a shouting crowd and,
> in the middle, MacLeod of Assynt and
> his greater prisoner—Montrose.[3]

In 'Among scholars', MacCaig describes walking with a few men (unnamed, but probably including Charlie Ross and A.K. MacLeod), lugging a boat:

> We left the boat in the hayfield at Inveruplan:
> The tractor would get it. A moon was coming up
> Over the roof and under it a Tilley lamp
> Hissed in its yellow self. We took our noise
> Into the room and shut it in with us
> Where, till light broke on a boat foundered in dew,
> I drank down drams in a company of scholars
> With exploding songs and a three-days ache in my shoulder.

MacCaig never read his own poetry at the ceilidhs. He just incited others to sing or play while he helped to reduce the whisky stocks. He never did poetry readings at Lochinver although he did readings all over Scotland. At Lochinver, which he continued to visit every year, almost until the end of his life, he had no wish to be in the public eye. In fact he was regarded very much as one of the 'locals' because he had been going there for so long. He was not treated by the people there as 'the great poet' and given a lot of attention from the media as happened in Edinburgh. This is no doubt partly the reason he liked going there! On the other hand—a common enough thing in some Highland communities—acquaintances, as opposed to friends, could be fairly tentative about talking to him.

Another occasional activity in Lochinver was country dancing in the old village hall. In 'Country dance' the fiddler is a man who held the fiddle with the right hand. In fact he was one of a whole family who had a fault in their wrist and they had to play the fiddle bowing with their left hand. MacCaig knew of another old man who ate tobacco. He amalgamated them into one old man, for the sake of the poem.

This poem gives a strong effect of combining colour, sound and music. It is full of life and lively touches—'whirled', 'flew', 'the jig bounced, the grace notes sparkled'. MacCaig is ignoring conventional reality and producing the surreal from a common event. It is the room that is dancing, the dancers produce 'gaiety' which turns into streamers flying in the air. Finally the poet sees a lesson or moral in the old fiddler and, taking a rise as usual out of ministers, he tells us that he has a pulpit in his mind into which, like a preacher, he climbs to pronounce solemnly on matters of importance: but before he can get going on his sermon, the spell is broken and the dance ends. The outcome is similar to 'Walking to Inveruplan' in that the poet is about to make a statement of devastating import when something happens and he doesn't!

Over the years, MacCaig sent the MacLeods each book of poetry as it appeared, autographed with his name. They had a mutual friend whom they called 'Boydie' (Mr Alex Boyd). MacLeod and 'Boydie' had to admit defeat in trying to understand some of the early poems. They told MacCaig so. He himself was aware of this and tried for many years to become more clear—engaged, as he said, in 'the long haul to lucidity'. For instance, in his poem 'Hogmanay' the language is simple, the message direct and the effect instantaneous!

> Murdo gave the cock meal
> damped with whisky. It stood
> on tiptoe, crowed eight times
> and fell flat on its beak.
>
> Later, Murdo, after the fifth verse
> of *The Isle of Mull*,
> fell, glass in hand,
> flat on his back—doing in six hours
> what the cock had done
> in two minutes.
>
> I was there. And now I see
> the cock crowing with Murdo's face

and Murdo's wings flapping
as down he went.

It was a long way home.

9. | Some Assynt Poems

In *A Round of Applause* (1962), MacCaig is beginning to produce more and more of his 'Assynt' poems—also the poems are becoming clearer and more spare.

In 'Memory two ways' he looks back on past holidays in Assynt and sees himself ten years earlier walking along a road past Loch an Ordain. He thinks how odd it would be if he, ten years younger, could see himself now:

> If he could see his fellow,
>
> His ten years older brother,
> How many roads, all corners,
> He'd have to look along
> To find him here, dark figure...

He liked to play with the concept of time.[1] In many poems he speaks of the inability of time to defeat the strength of memory and also of the sense of timelessness—of the unimportance of time—which he finds out on the hills and wild areas of Assynt.

There is a pastoral feel to some of the poetry of the sixties. In 'Spraying sheep':

> The dogs run on the ruined walls,
> Swinging their tongues, their minds all sheep.
> The zinc bath winks, the stirrup pump
> Guzzles the primrose one foot deep.

This poem acquires pace from the quick, sketchy descriptions. 'Sheep dipping, Achmelvich' is a similar pastoral poem, but has more evidence of the humour of his later poems. In it he makes fun of the sheep and their penchant for following one another willy-nilly. The shepherd chucks the first one into the sheep dip and she swims slowly through it. The rest follow her 'in the green turned suds'. They get out at the other end and

> With outraged cries

They waterfall uphill, spread out and stand
Dribbling salt water into flowers' eyes.

The poem is full of a sensuous richness of sounds, movements of water and
sheep, and the smell of soda; MacCaig catches the heavy, awkward actions of the
sheep in their fleecy coats wallowing in the green suds and then getting out rather
huffily and hurt at the other end, not pleased with what has happened, in the rather
sulky way so typical of sheep. Here we have the 'clinical eye', that misses nothing but
then combines with the 'artistic eye' to create a satisfying poem.

In 'Fetching cows', MacCaig is writing in his later, simpler style. Here he catches
very strongly the impression one gets on watching cows—their slow movements,
deviations to eat grass, their slouching walk. The cows are easy to control, so the
collie, used to rounding up sheep, is a bit bored with them. The poet notices how 'A
haycart squats prickeared against the sky'; the sun sets. It is a gentle poem, evocative
of the slow easy tempo of life in the West Highlands.

Another pastoral poem is 'Two shepherds'. Here MacCaig compares two friends
and their different methods of rounding up their sheep, the one full of sound and
fury, the other silent and subtle and apparently making little effort. He considers
them to be poets in their own 'languages':

Two poets—
Dionysian,
Appollonian
and the sheep in the pen.

Hill walking to get to a loch for fishing took up a lot of his time on holiday. The
sights and sounds of the landscapes of Assynt appear to have sunk into his subconscious. Poem after poem contains images of the mountains, the bog myrtle and
thyme with their heady scent, the sudden screaming appearance of a bird, the craggy
look of the hills, their resistance to his climbing feet, their god-like remoteness and
majesty, the freakish weather of the north west with its sudden mists and squalls and
gifts of beautiful days.

MacCaig immersed himself in these scenes in his holidays and, strangely, wrote
nothing at all about them at the time. All this was collected up in his memory and
written about often months, sometimes years, later in his quiet sitting room in
Edinburgh.

'Above Inverkirkaig' is a poem which could be a twin to 'Walking to Inveruplan'.
Again the poet is out at night walking around. The first section is very evocative of
MacCaig's way of thinking about himself and landscape—describing how landscape
affects him, stirring deep feelings of exultation and love.

I watch, across a loch
where seatrout are leaping,
Suilven and Cul Mor, my

> mountains of mountains,
> looming and pachydermatous in the thin light
> of a clear half moon. Something swells
> in my mind, in my self, as though
> I were about to be enlarged,
> to enclose informations and secrets
> that lie just beyond me that I would utter
> in one short, stupendous sentence, to the everlasting
> benefit of mankind and landscapes and me—
> a pregnant feeling that is, naturally, caused
> by love.

Again, as in 'Walking to Inveruplan' the moonlight gives him the feeling that he is about to understand the riddles of existence but this proves beyond his grasp, the dream fades.

There are many 'mountain' poems. 'Looking down on Glen Canisp' describes a hot 'heavy' day:

> Even the ravens
> have sunk into the sandstone cliffs
> of Suilven, that are dazed blue
> and fuzz into the air around them—
> as my mind does, till I hear
> a thin far clatter and
> look down to where two stags
> canter across the ford, splashing up before them
> antlers of water.

His images of birds are particularly beautiful. In the 'mountain' poems we come across, for example, several references to ravens. They sink into sandstone cliffs (see above), are puffed out of 'Quinag, that tall/huddle of anvils'[2] and play up and down on the 'chute' of the wind which goes up the cliff face of Suilven.[3]

In one particular bird poem, 'Heron', he concentrates on one thing, on the heron and on describing it. The poem does not say anything of earth-shattering moment; MacCaig details its characteristic appearance, movements, eating habits, how it spears its food, its flying, etc. But here is no boring 'biology notes' type of poem, here is a work of art; the bird is a marvel of movement. His heron is a 'personality'—it has a presence and invests the hills and water around it with significance just by being there as the centre piece for the eye. He describes it with a gentle, comic love—the bird is just a bit like a prim aunt stepping out in Princes Street.

In a rather fussy poem, 'Starlings', he looks at the birds in a tree and tries to decide what they remind him of. A series of pictures present themselves—mediaeval scholars, busybodies in a bazaar, clockwork fossils. The birds finally fly off, land on the grass and become

> bustling monks
> tilling their green precincts.

He had a particular gift which few people have in such a developed state for seeing correspondences between one creature and another, or one object and another. He maintained that this was not 'imagination'. One friend called it a 'seeing eye' and said it was a Gaelic trait. An example is found in 'Now and for ever' where the poet looks

> at the sea, at a rock where
> a cormorant, wings half spread, stands
> like a man proving to his tailor
> how badly his suit fits.

To MacCaig the north west highlands had an almost 'holy' quality about them. In 'No accident' he used Biblical imagery to describe his feelings for the 'heaven' of being on Suilven. He remarked on occasion that 'the mountains are my religion'. In this poem he says that Suilven is a type of heaven which one can only enter when one is in a state of grace and that he himself one day came to such a state through being crippled by a twisted knee. The effects of this were that, because walking was painful, and he had to slow down, he became more aware than usual of the mountain's heaven-like qualities.

Nearly all the examples of the use of religious imagery come from the books published before *A Man in my Position*, i.e. from his 'Middle Period' poetry.

'Byre' starts off by comparing the roof of the byre with heaven. The mice of 'Haycock, Achiltibuie' have now acquired a new status. This time they play the role, not of sinners, but of an angelic chorus, squeaking 'small hosannahs' and scratching on the golden pavements of heaven beside the crystal river of the guttering. Here we have MacCaig's love of elevating insignificant animals to play roles of importance in his mind's eye.

In the second stanza he comes down to earth and describes kittens playing in 'the world below', catching their wild and unpredictable way of darting about. Finally the heroines of the piece, the cows, swagbellied goddesses of love, come in. The choir of mice falls silent but the kittens play on, unimpressed.

But he is by no means entirely awestruck by the 'holy' things of life. He cannot resist poking fun at great men and in 'Holy moon' (*RT:* not in *CP*) he gets on to Raphael. MacCaig paints a silver-tinted picture of moonlight in his room. The moon transforms the room and transports him in time back to the Middle Ages, to a holier age, where faith was strong. He hears sounds of the Middle Ages, of flagellation and rapt singing—evoking the days when men mortified the flesh in order to draw closer to God. Having built up this powerful image, he then explodes it all with the line, 'Raphael did a quick job on the sky', reducing Raphael to the status of a tax-dodging house painter working for a friend of a friend in the evenings.

Some critics say that MacCaig is too 'jokey' ever to be termed a great poet, that

Suilven near Lochinver, MacCaig's 'mountain of mountains'

he cannot resist the tendency to insert jokes into the most lyrical of descriptions. But he in fact writes to please himself, not with one eye on a place in Parnassus. He has frequently remarked that he does not care what critics say of him, that he writes because he feels 'hungry' for a poem. In 'Holy Moon' he is being rather like Wallace Stevens, painting a picture of great beauty with touches of irony but giving us no explanation, no deep truth to ponder on. The poem is an object of art—a thing in itself without a 'meaning' unless perhaps to describe the transformative powers of moonlight.

Another poem called simply 'Moon' is one of his most artistic and visual poems. All the images are in black and gold and silver and there are sensuous references to the moon as a wanton woman wandering the landscape and clouds:

> She stirs light into the sea
> With a long gold finger
> And lies, naked and tawny,
> On innumerable shores.

There is almost a feeling of magic in the last stanza:

> And skulls of sleeping
> Women grow radiant.

10. Free Verse and Two Visits to New York

MacCaig began to write in free verse in the mid sixties. The first book in which such poems appear in any number is *Surroundings*, 1966. He considered this book to be a kind of turning point.

In 1976, in *Chapman*, he described this move:

> There came an evening…eight or nine years ago, when I broodily sat down to write a poem and to my surprise the little thing was fledged in free verse. I of course produced more of the same and got very interested in the techniques of this, to me, new form. Whoever it was—was it Graves, or Auden?—who said, in contempt of free verse, that it was like playing tennis without a net was talking through a hole in his own practice. The formal structure of a metrical, rhymed poem may be in some respects a restricting straitjacket, but it also keeps you from flailing your arms about in meaningless, shapeless gestures, and it's my belief that to write a formally good poem in free verse is more difficult than to mosaic away with iambs and feminine rhymes. How many free verse poems are ruined by the lack of a through-going rhythm to articulate the whole and by line-endings which are purely arbitrary and serve no functional purpose whatever.[1]

The poems are becoming more concerned with the human condition in this collection. There are several poems on semi-political themes—'Progress', 'Smuggler' and 'Leader of men'. In 'Progress' he writes:

> When the armies marched off
> cursing the criminal stupidity of their leaders
> to fight for the glory and prosperity
> of the motherland,
> the leaders
> did their bit
> by putting the prices up…

A marked quality of MacCaig, becoming increasingly evident in his poetry from this point in his life on, was his independence of spirit, his refusal to toe any party

63

line. He had a strong dislike of politicians and anyone else who tried to tell him how to think. In an interview on T.V. with Alistair Moffat in 1982 he pointed out:

MacCaig: All the poets in Scotland are Nationalists.
Moffat: Why do you think that is?
MacCaig: Because they despise politics and what on earth has Scottish Nationalism to do with politics?
Moffat: What about your own politics? Are you a Scottish Nationalist?
MacCaig: I vote for the Scottish Nationalists. I have never voted for anyone else. But, driven on by the sure conviction that they would not get in. But I wanted a certain number of Scottish Nationalists down yonder just to be a kind of horsefly on the black backside of Westminster.

Later in the same interview he continued in fine abrasive style:

MacCaig: When politicians are speaking they use words purely for their emotional, 'penny in the slot' reaction. Most people have unexamined ideas and unexamined emotions even. So that when a fellow says 'S.D.P., clap, clap handies!' if you are that sort of fool, or 'Boo, boo, boo' if you are that sort of fool, they don't know what these politicians believe. Do you know why? Because neither do the politicians! They only use words emotively. Unexamined ideas and unexamined emotions are the cause of most of the trouble in the world, and poetry makes you regard words very carefully in both these aspects and you don't get these idiotic 'penny in the slot' responses.
Moffat: Who would you say are the main people to blame in society for evincing these 'penny in the slot' responses? You mentioned politicians.
MacCaig: Oh, religious chaps of whatever kind.[2]

He had a hatred of glib pronouncements. In 'My Way of It' he wrote:

Poetry teaches a man to do more than observe merely factual errors and measurable truths. It trains him to have a shrewd nose for the fake, the inflated, the imprecise and the dishonest. So it compels him to resist stock responses, because it compels him to examine the emotional significance, as well as the rational significance, of whatever comes under his notice.

He put this very succinctly in a poem, 'Smuggler':

> Watch him when he opens
> his bulging words—justice,
> fraternity, freedom, internationalism, peace,
> peace, peace. Make it your custom
> to pay no heed
> to his frank look, his visas, his stamps

and signatures. Make it
your duty to spread out their contents
in a clear light.

Nobody with such luggage
has nothing to declare.

In 'Assisi', a poem which he wrote following a trip to Italy, he is concerned with
man's inhumanity to man.[3] The people here making the 'stock response' are a group
of tourists who ignore a beggar at the door of the church. MacCaig disliked the way
people react to others according to their status, not their worth as human beings,
automatically ignoring the poor and automatically listening to the powerful.

He also had a dislike of dry academic people. 'To a pragmatist' (S, not in CP) is
interesting because here we see the beginnings of MacCaig as an 'anti-academic'
poet: he shows his dislike of the man whose subject has become cut and dried like old
peat and holds no uncertainties or possibilities. MacCaig liked life to be mysterious
and inexplicable and hated those who packaged experience tidily and pragmatically.

But MacCaig could turn his brilliant spotlight on himself also. The book starts
with 'Metaphysical me' (S, not in CP). In this poem MacCaig sends up his own
propensities to be metaphysical in his writing:

He fawned on objects.
He serenaded the dust in the streets
And made himself ridiculous about fish.
There wasn't an interruption of space
He didn't flatter, saying
It was an interruption of time.
Politicians
Didn't understand him.

Surroundings also contains a continuation of the Assynt poems. So amongst what
appears to be an awakening conscience about the ills of the world to the extent, not
just of thinking but writing about them, we have 'Near midnight', 'Loch Roe', and
'Looking down on Glen Canisp'.

Surroundings was a Poetry Book Society Choice for 1966. In that same year
MacCaig was invited to attend a Writers' Conference at Long Island University,
New York, to read his poetry and talk about it. He found the New York academics
a very hospitable group of people. One of them with whom he became friendly
discovered that he was living in a hotel and immediately invited him to stay in his
own home for the duration of the visit. He found that there was much less of a divide
between staff and students in America than in Britain. They socialised freely, visited
one another's homes, drank in the same bars at the University.

He attended quite a few parties. A friend had warned him before he went that
parties in New York could be homicidal! But he did not find them so. Always a keen

party-goer anyway, he enjoyed them immensely and spent much time talking to academics and students. MacCaig:

> The American women take an equal part in any conversation. Why not? Often they said things that were more interesting and witty than the men. Over here I sometimes have to say 'Give the lady a shot' when two men are talking while a lady is present.[4]

He recalled an incident which occurred away from the sheltered groves of Academe:

> First time I went into a bar with a New York academic, an extremely nice man, we got a couple of whiskies. I bought the next round. I said 'Two whiskies please.' The barman gave me a hard look. When I got them I said 'Thank you very much.' Again he gave me a hard look. I asked my friend if I had said something wrong. He pointed out that I had said 'please' and 'thank you' and that this was looked on as very odd in fast moving, no nonsense New York. The waiters in the restaurants slap the food down in front of you. If you say 'please' and 'thank you' they think you are taking the mickey.[5]

He was cosseted in New York in the academic world and did not meet the ordinary or extraordinary New Yorkers themselves. However, he did do the usual tourist trips, visiting Battery Park, the Metropolitan Museum, Times Square and Brooklyn.

In 'Circle Line' he describes going on a half day guided tour by ferry round Manhattan Island. The guide, who was full of gossip and blue jokes, kept disappearing for a drink. The landmarks were 'shot' by the tourist cameras, particular attention being paid by all to Frank Sinatra's penthouse. The poem is superficial and jokey, emphasising the 'brief glimpse' type of tour, the fleeting impression, the particular tourist mentality that demands a constant change of scene and ever more landmarks to photograph. MacCaig here took on the voice of such a tourist:

> We...
> ...turn south down the Hudson...
> ...ignoring
> the Statute of Liberty. We've seen her
> already. We've had her.

MacCaig found New York a rough, tough city; a very exciting, bizarre place; a city which overwhelmed one's senses with its noise, its drive, its rich and poor, its materialism, its drama; its horror and its breathtaking ability to stun one's senses. He was much impressed and affected by it and wrote several poems about how he felt, shot through with his own brand of acid comment and humour:

> The sun goes up on Edinburgh,
> Manhattan goes up on the sun.[6]

'Hotel room, 12th floor' is perhaps the most famous of MacCaig's New York poems and appears in several anthologies. In it he compares the world of New York to the world of the Wild West. The poem shows a battle going on between the forces of man-made New York and the forces of Nature. It is a battle between the lights of Manhattan and the approach of darkness and midnight. As the two forces fight for control, the streets of the city are turned into a Wild West scenario of 'glittering canyons and gulches' with police cars and ambulances touring the streets making warwhooping noises as they rush to scenes of violence. The stockades of New York are unable to keep out the dark forces of both nature and of evil.

This theme of New York as a city of danger and clashing forces of good and evil, light and dark, superficial calm and underlying tension, is brought out very clearly in another poem, 'Brooklyn cop'. Here MacCaig sketches the man in a sort of 'Toulouse-Lautrec' style with broad exaggerated brush strokes, showing all his human qualities. The poem vibrates with an underlying sense of danger. The cop is a man of controlled violence stalking trouble. There is a sense of movement, of tension, of striving for control in the poem. One can visualise the gorilla-like cop as a dancer in a strange ritual ballet. This huge, ugly man moves carefully over the 'thin tissue of violence' which could so easily break, throwing him into a fight, injury or even death.

> Should the tissue tear, should he plunge through
> into violence, what clubbings, what
> gunshots between Phoebe's Whamburger
> and Louie's Place.

An interesting poem which came out of MacCaig's New York experiences is 'Writers' Conference, Long Island University'. In this he looks at life with a kind of reductive vision, showing that all men are as grass, that most of life is 'froth and bubble' and that all men in the end are merely mortal. The recurring theme of death runs through many of his poems—a West Highland obsession with death, with the fact that 'in life we are in death', that even at the most glittering occasion, the finger of death can touch the pulse beat.

In the poem MacCaig captures an academic occasion, contrasting the scintillating language of the speakers with the old, tarnished glitter of the hall which was presumably once used as a place for dancing or for song and dance shows.

> ...All round and overhead, glitters
> a poor man's Sistine Chapel
> of gold scrolls and foiled trumpets, of
> pumped-up Cupids and Muses...

He wonders what has become of the 'hoofers, clowns and galvanised tap-dancers' and then points out in a rather macabre way how both academics and dancers will end up silent 'under the sibilating language of the grass',[7] although the ideas of the academics will live on in human thought.

While he was at the Conference, he met Professor John Weston from Amherst College, Massachusetts. He invited MacCaig to visit the University at Amherst so he spent half of his time in New York and half at Amherst.

While on the 1966 trip, MacCaig gave some talks on MacDiarmid and this interested the students and they asked MacCaig to bring him over. So the next year he went back with MacDiarmid. They flew to America on 20 April, 1967, for a three week stay. They gave talks and read their poetry to University students in New York and Massachusetts. There was a great interest in America in Scottish writing. It was appreciated for its quality, directness and vigour. It seemed to the Americans to be different from current modes.

At one of the lectures they gave in Massachusetts, they were both to read their poetry. MacCaig talked about and read his own poetry first. Then MacDiarmid got up. He wrote, of course, largely in Scots, a language which he had adopted along with the name of MacDiarmid. MacDiarmid always maintained that Scots was a much more expressive and poetic language than English which he thought 'soft'. Getting to his feet, he announced emphatically, 'My good friend Norman has made a good contribution to English literature but NOT ME!'

In MacCaig's next volume of poems, *Rings on a Tree* (1968), there appeared the series of New York poems. Asked later whether 'Brooklyn cop' was a rare example of a character sketch, MacCaig disagreed as to the rarity of this type of poem: 'I do more [character] sketches as time goes on. I may not name them. There are quite a number about particular people. More than people think.'[8]

For instance, 'Gaelic Poet' (*MP*, not in *CP*) concerns Sorley MacLean and 'Confession' concerns MacDiarmid. These both appeared at the same time and in the same book, *A Man in My Position* (1969), as well as 'Mrs Grant', which is very obviously a character sketch.

Occasional poems about America continued to appear after *Rings on a Tree*. One example is 'Power dive'. MacCaig said of this poem that it is 'a fable—a warning not to get too rich'. It is a tiny, shocking story in two parts. It starts with a set of seven lines, depicting a very rich man building and developing a house and garden and (his pride and joy), a swimming pool 'that glittered like ancient Rome'. The second set of three short terse lines says:

> It was just before he hit the water
> in his first dive that he glimpsed
> the triangular fin cutting the surface.

'19th floor nightmare, New York' appeared in *The Equal Skies*.[9] This, like 'Power dive' is a short narrative, rapid in pace and with a shocking and comic end. A girl has been sleeping a deep and drunken sleep and has a nightmare from which she wakes, screaming. She is staying, appropriately enough, in the Mandragora Hotel; 'mandragora' being the name of a narcotic drug derived from the mandrake root, which root is thought to resemble human form and to 'shriek when plucked'. MacCaig here uses the connotations of the word 'mandragora' and the New York setting and finally blends with these a sinister 'eye of King Kong' image. He has quite a few of these 'shock ending' poems, possibly written to entertain audiences at live readings as much as for their qualities as poems 'on the page'.

Maurice Lindsay said of the poetry of the 1960s:

> Metaphysics, though a very Scottish preoccupation, do not by themselves shape a poet, and it is the combination of that intellectual toughness of strand they provide matched with the vigorous colours of MacCaig's imagery in his middle and best period that has resulted in his producing some of the finest poetry in English in our native literature.[10]

Rings on a Tree, published in 1968, is perhaps the most brilliant of MacCaig's books. The inclusion of the New York sequence of poems is striking because they are very much a departure from the norm for MacCaig, who usually confined his poems about places to Assynt and Edinburgh. But it also contains 'Rhu Mor', one of his finest 'sea' poems and 'Balances' which concerns the role of the poet in today's world.

'Balances' in fact sums up very briefly an aspect of MacCaig's philosophy. In the first part he argues for the importance to him of describing the beauties of nature, despite the bad state of the world:

> Because I see the world poisoned
> by cant and brutal self-seeking,
> must I be silent about
> the useless waterlily, the dunnock's nest
> in the hedgeback?

In the second and third sections he argues for the importance of individual love as opposed to a concern with 'ideas' or 'fellow workers'. The final part of the poem sums it up:

> There are more meanings than those
> in text books of economics
> and a part of the worst slum
> is the moon rising over it
> and eyes weeping and
> mouths laughing.

The poem 'Old maps and new' sets out similar ideas to those in 'Balances', showing how in the world it is not just the 'important' things that matter; the trivial, the little kindness, should also be noted by the poet:

> In the Leader's pocket,

wrapped in the plans for the great offensive,
are sweets for the children
and a crumpled letter.

In a radio interview William Carrocher discussed with MacCaig the difference between 'frivolous' and 'light-hearted' and MacCaig leapt to the defence of light poetry as opposed to heavily meaningful poetry about suffering and despair.[11]

In his 'My way of it' article MacCaig said, in defence of 'trivial' subject matter:

I also hatefully reject the limiting notion, bannered and free-floated most spec-tacularly by A. Alvarez, that, the times being what they are, the only poetry possible is a poetry of extremes, scribbled frantically on your way back from a mental hospital to commit suicide. Of course there is poetry to be written from the far edge of consciousness, of suffering, of despair. But into my, and your, five ports of knowledge come many cargoes and we should unship the lot. If art is to be concerned only with the tragic or, even, only with the huge concepts of death, alienation, love, loss of Eden, and what the devil is Time anyway, a vast amount of the great art of the past will have to be rejected as 'irrelevant'. There's conceit for you. I also detest the notion that all art is a therapeutic expression of inner, psychological tensions, of the quarrel with ourselves whose expression Yeats thought produces poetry as opposed to rhetoric. Of course that is true of a great deal of art. But what about the other great deal, whose cause, purpose and effect is pure celebration of a woman or a chair or a landscape? Are we to dismiss these as trivial? If so, I have written a good many trivial poems...

11. | Edinburgh University

In 1967 MacCaig became Writer in Residence at Edinburgh University. He worked there for two years, the first person to hold such a post at a Scottish university. Students who were interested in writing could consult him about their work, get their writing criticised, take part in 'workshops' and hear talks about writers from the Writer in Residence. He was asked by a journalist in August, 1968, just following his reappointment for a further year, what was the object of the appointment. He replied, 'Partly to give tired old hacks like me more time to get on with their own writing'![1]

He was given a small room like an office or tutorial room, Isabel was given membership of the Ladies Tea Club and that was that. It was up to him what he did thereafter. He stuck a notice on the door advertising a meeting and inviting anybody interested to come along. Eleven people turned up, including nine Americans. As he put it, 'The dour and sluggish Scots were waiting to see what happened!'

The Americans, of course, already had a tradition of Writers in Residence at their Universities and there were also one or two Writers in Residence in England. The group, which met once a week, gradually built up and the Americans became outnumbered.

Valerie Gillies (nee Simmons), the poet, was a second year English student. She had already been writing poetry for some time prior to this and went to a poetry reading one evening at the University. This ended up with questions and developed into a discussion about T. S. Eliot, whom most of the students had been taught to revere. A voice from the back of the room suddenly delivered the most tremendous downgrading of Eliot ever heard. Valerie realised that it was MacCaig and thought him a most iconoclastic person. She followed this up by going to see him with some of her poems. But in his office she found a very different person from the one who shot down Eliot in flames—a gentle, precise critic, eager to help and encourage.

MacCaig was interested in fostering creativity. Many students and a few members of staff began to consult him individually. Lannette Kennish (nee Miller), also a poet, has recalled:

I would give him poems hot off the typewriter. Once he handed some back with his deep-sea smile and said, 'You've found your voice.' I was grateful for the time he gave us.[2]

MacCaig, in a B.B.C. interview with Roderick Watson, was later to say:

I thought it was impossible to teach anybody to write poetry. I still think it in a way. I used to have a quotation:

> The feathered tribes on pinions skim the air,
> Not so the mackerel and still less the bear.

So if you didn't have it in you, you know, you could never do it. But I found that when the students came with their poems, so long as I didn't try to get them to write in the way that I thought they should write, they improved extraordinarily. For two simple reasons: they had somebody to show their poems to who was interested and so they wrote more and I went through their poems with a tooth-comb made of plush and so they started writing more self critically and if you add these two things together, writing more, and more self critically, their improvement was extraordinary.[3]

He enjoyed working at the University but did, however, occasionally regret man's inbuilt tendency to commit immortal verse. He found that one got people, all too numerous, who thought they could write poetry and who would pour it out and then load it on to someone else to criticise and give an opinion; that there was an unstoppable flow of bad poetry going on all the time and that, of all the poems written, only a tiny percentage actually ever got printed.

One particular foreign man used to bring in poetry by the yard. MacCaig has recalled that he handed him a huge bundle of pages covered in poetry to have a look at.

'Did you write poetry in your own language before you came to Britain?' MacCaig asked him.

'Oh no', he said 'Much too difficult. Writing poetry in English is easy. Will I write you three?'[4]

MacCaig was interested in introducing the students to American and European poetry. Occasionally he would invite well known writers to the Wednesday lunch time seminars, e.g. Sydney Goodsir Smith, Alexander Scott, Hugh MacDiarmid and George Mackay Brown. He also introduced the students to many new poets seldom looked at in conventional courses of English Literature—European, Russian, Swedish and American poets (including Bob Dylan). He liked poetry with realism, with a philosophic nut in it or a 'bite'.

In MacCaig's poetry at this time there began to be heard faint murmurings of an anti-academic nature. He wrote several such poems. What he objected to was the narrow academic who could only talk about his own field of work and who seemed to live in a hermetically sealed box, cut off from other spheres of thought and experience. As far as MacCaig was concerned, these 'narrow' academics were one thing and true scholars quite another.

In 'An academic' there is a tone of cutting sarcasm—MacCaig at his most lethal:

> You sit at your fat desk, starching
> your brains...
>
> I'm a simple man—I believe
> you were born, I believe it
> against all the evidence.

He depicts a man totally lacking in joie de vivre, sensitivity, sexual passion, adventure. This theme is repeated with variations in some other poems, for example, 'University staff club'. 'Types' (*MP*, not in *CP*) concerns several academics all looking distantly at 'life' but never really getting involved:

> His colleague dips a toe
> into the meniscus of four faiths
> and betrays them all. If only
> he'd wet even his kneebones.

While he was at University, he was much in demand to give poetry readings in Edinburgh. He appeared on occasion with the 1320 Club, a Scottish Nationalist group who met in Edinburgh. At one of their ceilidhs in 1969[5] during the Edinburgh Festival, so many people turned up that not only did devotees sit at the feet of MacCaig, they were more or less stood on by him!

At this time he was reading a lot of what he called 'snapshot' poems—short descriptive poems that were fairly easy to take in at first hearing—often humorous and with a 'sting in the tail', such as 'Wild oats':

> Every day I see from my window
> pigeons, up on a roof ledge—the males
> are wobbling gyroscopes of lust.
>
> Last week a stranger joined them, a snowwhite
> pouting fantail,
> Mae West in the Women's Guild.
> What becks, what croo-croos, what
> demented pirouetting, what a lack
> of moustaches to stroke.
>
> The females—no need to be one of them
> to know
> exactly what they were thinking—pretended
> she wasn't there

and went dowdily on with whatever
pigeons do when they're knitting.

A new book of poems called *A Man in My Position* appeared in 1969. Here we get the mature man of 59 looking at the world. 'No end, no beginning' concerns the constant renewal of life.

Some of his most humorous and most telling poems are sketches of women. Often a woman is depicted as an oddity, or in a comic way. 'Venus fly-trap' is a horrific poem about a predatory woman. MacCaig: 'I think I had a particular lady in mind. A vampire! I watched what she did to men.'[6]

'Mrs Grant' is a cross between a short story and a character sketch. The woman emerges fully fledged from the poem—no misty shadow. He took as his original an old lady who was an alcoholic and lived in rather bizarre circumstances in a small village near South Queensferry. He paints a grim picture of a person disintegrating under the self-imposed burden of drink and drugs, but the poem is also spiced with humour which paradoxically builds up the sense of horror—a good example of how he seems to latch onto odd and eccentric people, whom most others would ignore if possible. (See also 'Street preacher', the dwarf in 'Assisi' and 'Brooklyn cop'.)

In all his poems about relationships and events and places, he distorts and exaggerates situations and personalities to achieve effects. In 'Bluestocking' he turns his merciless spyglass on a woman academic who asks him questions. The poem begins:

Anything I say
she judiciously considers with
quotations and references.
What weight is anything I say
when in the other scale she puts
Aristotle and Chomsky?[7]

The lady is so learned, she seems unapproachable. She would even cry in an intellectual way—her tears quoting her nose! Here he uses a common theme: the difficulty he has in understanding the opposite sex. He resents her 'intellectualism' which he considers a sort of veneer:

If only I could blue pencil
this bluestocking
and get down to
the original script.

In the poem 'Names' he does a sort of conjuring trick. Often he starts to write a poem on one subject and it then turns into something else altogether. This one begins with the poet looking into a shallow pool and naming all the strange little fish that swim there—'rock goby, lumpsucker, father lasher'. He then says how easy it is to name a person or a fish but that he can no more understand the individual (presumably a lady) he is thinking of than he can understand the nature of a fish:

> ...you have selves as secret from me
> as blenny or butterfish.
>
> ...we move always sideways to each other, like
> a velvet fiddler and a porcelain crab.

One or two of the poems about women are based on fantasy. He enjoyed conjuring up his beautiful vision, the mysterious lady who drifts into the bar through the smoke and fumes. In 'Fishermen's pub' he recalls the 'silken lady' of Alexander Blok.

> ...Remember, in one of the Russias,
> Alexander Blok drunk beyond his own mercy—
>
> How he saw, through the smoke and the uproar,
> His 'silken lady' come in and fire
> The fire within him? I found myself staring
>
> For mine, for that wild miraculous presence
> That would startle the world new with her forgivingness,
> But nothing was there but sidling smokewreaths...

MacDiarmid in his poem 'A Drunk Man Looks at the Thistle' introduced a lyric adapted from Alexander Blok and MacCaig's poem refers to this same incident. Nancy Gish says of the MacDiarmid lyric:

It crystallises a moment of intense realisation or awareness. Opening with images of the moon looking over a spring night and a pub, it depicts the nightly presence among the drunken crew of a mysterious, dreamlike woman. Who she is or what she means is never said, but her power lies in an exotic fascination. She is a 'silken leddy' who 'darkly moves'. From her robes a 'rooky dwamin' (misty swooning) perfume comes.[8]

MacCaig's poems about women seem to get more comic as the poet ages—see 'Antique shop window', 'Gone are the days' and 'Flirt'. 'Cold song' is a very comic, very cryptic poem. He is making fun of his own and other people's ways of looking at a pretty young girl and of how they each perceive her differently:

> The doctor gazed
> at the sack of guts passing
> and saw
> my pretty girl...

In many poems he describes a woman close to him to whom he returns again and again as to a glowing hearth; she is to him 'home', peace and security. An example of this is 'True ways of knowing'.

'Prisoner' (*MP*, not in *CP*) is a remarkable poem about being imprisoned in a very close relationship with a woman. It is comic in vein, particularly at the start. The lady thinks that he belongs to her and that he is an 'object' who can be trotted out and shown off to friends whenever the whim takes her. The poet disagrees with this and goes on to point to the lady's dependence on him. In fact he claims it is she who is imprisoned by him. With a final paradox he turns a somersault on his whole theory:

> It's not my helplessness that makes me your prisoner,
> it's yours.

He begins to let suffering appear in the poems, to allow more emotion to surface. One of his most famous poems is 'Visiting hour'. This is about Isabel when she was in hospital in Edinburgh. She almost died, and at the time the poem is set was near death. But she recovered. There is a starkness about it that goes with the life and death feeling of being in hospital. There is also a tremendous sense of tension and yet it is achieved by understatement. The poem depicts a man pushing back fear and despair from his mind:

> I will not feel, I will not
> feel, until
> I have to.

MacCaig hated displays of emotion almost to the extent of being accused of coldness.

No dramatic description is given of his very ill wife, just the image of her withered hand that 'trembles on its stalk' and yet here we see the life force about to break down, the eyelids too heavy to raise and only the 'glass fang' in her arm and the thin flow of fluid through it keeping life going. And then MacCaig dramatically sees himself as it were through her eyes:

> She smiles a little at this
> black figure in her white cave
> who clumsily rises
> in the round swimming waves of a bell
> and dizzily goes off...

A Man in My Position contains two very sad poems on the death of his sister, Frances—'Spilled salt' and 'In my mind'. In 'Spilled salt' he delineates grief. The great thing about his sister was that she 'noticed him'. She was a loving presence in his life, she bolstered his ego and so when she died, he grieved over the loss of this close companion:

> She whose look
> gave me the size
> I thought I was
>
> became spilled salt;
> for she
> had stopped noticing.

In his next book *The White Bird* appears the poem 'Memorial'. This concerns the death of a woman close to him (probably Frances). It conveys a feeling rather akin to the sensation one gets on listening to an elegy being played on the cello. The first three lines sound in their rhythm like phrases of music:

> Everywhere she dies. Everywhere I go she dies.
> No sunrise, no city square, no lurking beautiful mountain
> but has her death in it...

He highlights the way the fact of someone dying re-echoes in the mind long after their actual death. The effect is so deep and fundamental that it cuts through other feelings:

> The silence of her dying sounds through
> The carousel of language...

In the final section the poet is transformed into a walking elegy, and the last lines, again like cello music, draw the intense feeling of the poem to a sorrowful close:

> Ever since she died
> she can't stop dying. She makes me
> her elegy. I am a walking masterpiece,
> a true fiction
> of the ugliness of death.
> I am her sad music.

12. The Wilds of Assynt

> Warm clay in the stone wants to come back to me.
> That Inchnadamph cliff is full of squeaking fossils.
> The sun sinks back to helium. The sea
> Boils before ice. Oh, the loud primevals![1]

MacCaig continued to return every summer to the wild and beautiful area of Assynt. He is perhaps *par excellence* a poet who celebrates the delights of the Western Highlands. By his poetry he has opened up not only a sparsely populated geographical area—Lochinver and its surroundings—but he has also turned a spotlight on its animals, birds and a landscape which many take for granted. The tourist rushing through the area does not see them, but the slow traveller on foot or bicycle can see these small miracles. Their amazing properties are heightened by MacCaig's uncanny ability not just to see them but to 'see' additional possibilities around them for fantasy, for the humanising of nature.

He is constantly seeing one thing in terms of another. A toad in a well is Buddha, a fern, its Bo-tree;[2] Suilven in a storm of wind makes a deep tremolo sound and becomes an organ to delight Bach himself;[3] the moon becomes a fast woman, shamelessly lying alongside a fence, pacing 'the smouldering magnesium of clouds' lying seductively on the shore 'naked and tawny'.[4]

The great pastime for both 'local' and holiday maker at Lochinver is fishing. Assynt is well supplied with lochs and lochans, and the Assynt Angling Club controls fishing on 35 lochs in the area. MacCaig used to join in with their competitions and he helped to run the Junior Club competitions. Always a keen fisherman, he would frequently walk long distances on his own or in company, often with Ewen, or occasionally with A.K., to reach remote lochs.

There is trout fishing in Loch Assynt, the largest loch in the area, and around remote Drumbeg, where there are at least twenty lochs. Going into the Drumbeg Hotel bar in the evening, one is liable to fall over a lot of fishermen who have stuffed themselves into the corners—it is the only crowded spot for miles around!

In an article in the *Listener*, November 1968, MacCaig described fishing in Assynt:

Clearly this is a marvellous landscape for walking through. And if you're a fisherman, the lochs are, most of them, so small and so close together you can wander about all one long day without seeing a soul, and come home with trout taken from six, eight, ten lochs. In most of them a trout weighing a pound would be a good fish, but there are some, whose names I seem to have forgotten for the moment, where they run much larger than that. My own personal best was six and three-quarter pounds. It came out of a loch, set in a landscape of crags and corries, that you could walk round in a quarter of an hour, and a number of deer, minute on the skyline above me, watched with interest as I played it.

Trout, salmon, sea-trout in the rivers; red deer, roe deer, otters, foxes, wild cats in the hills and woods; ravens, eagles, buzzards, hawks in the air—these are only the beginning of a long list of the creatures that add their enlivening interest to the landscape, and it has made no mention of the teeming life in the sea, and above it. Wherever one goes one is never very far from the sea—clean and pure, exploding on cliffs, poking inland as sea lochs or creeping up over sandy beaches almost as white as salt.

Over and over again in his Lochinver poems we come across him as a lone figure fishing or walking or climbing, miles from anywhere.

> Such comfortless places comfort me.
> Not my body but I am fed by these ravens
> And I'm nourished by the drib-drab waters
> That fingerling through the harsh deer grass.
> The tall cliffs unstun my mind...[5]

MacCaig frequently refers in his poetry, as here, to the way that his mind feeds on images. He told an interviewer once that he had a 'greedy and guzzling eye'. In 'Proud walkers' (*RT*, not in *CP*) he first depicts the way a storm can pounce down on the fisherman in his boat, bringing rain and wind of such ferocity that it raises an effect like curtains of water over the loch. In his mind's eye he then sees these curtains as the 'ominous naked ladies in a painting by Paul Delvaux'—and one can understand why MacCaig was attracted to Assynt if his imagination could conjure up such bizarre companions for his fishing trips!

His favourite mountain was Suilven, a curiously-shaped peak that sits like some vast sleeping Buddha on the wild lands just behind Lochinver itself. He frequently talks of Suilven in his poems.[6] It was a mountain which seemed to exert a magnetic force on him. Suilven is, in fact, a bit of a quick-change artiste. It can look very different according to the light and the clouds. It is a preposterous shape—a tower of sandstone from one angle and a long series of humps from another. Seen from the village of Elphin it looks like a remote monster, the last survivor of an ancient breed.

There is a reference to the great god Pan in 'Notations of ten summer minutes'. Pan seems in this poem to haunt the hills around MacCaig's Lochinver. A pantheistic, pagan streak runs through MacCaig's poetry—a love of the wild and the frightening elements in nature, a love of storms, and an intense close observation of the creatures and elements. A sense of nature in the raw, unadorned or prettified, pervades his work.

In the much earlier 'Spate in winter midnight', he evokes the fear stirred up in wild animals by the sound and fury of a stormy night. It is a poem full of pent up energy and a sense of lurking evil. His poems often contain very energetic images, a feeling of movement—there is an almost cinematic quality to them:

> Through Troys of bracken and Babel towers of rocks
> Shrinks now the looting fox.
> Fearful to touch the thudding ground
> And flattened to it by the mastering sound...[7]

This is a 'night' poem—the poet is out in the storm observing it or imagining he is doing so. Having built up this sense of fear and evil, he ends by pointing to one creature which is not frightened:

> ...the cold adder sleeps in his small bed,
> Curled neatly round his neat and evil head.

Pan also seems not far away in 'Goat', in which MacCaig describes a goat on a ledge almost as if it has human qualities and is laughing at him.[8]

It is said that sometimes wanderers in wild and lonely places are overcome by fear which seems to some from a supernatural source. One day, out on the hills, MacCaig had a strange, irrational experience. He went to fish a familiar loch, high up on Canisp, and, while he was getting his rod ready, he had a spooky feeling that there were 'presences' watching him. He forced himself to fish round the loch and was glad to leave it. He understood then what it meant to the inhabitants of the old Peloponnese to be in the company of Pan.

In the summer holidays of 1968, Valerie Gillies and a group of Norwegian students went to Sutherland. They stayed in the Youth Hostel in Achmelvich which is near MacCaig's cottage, and visited him. The first evening they called, MacCaig and a friend arrived back from fishing and Isabel cooked fresh trout for them all. The Norwegians were greatly impressed by the hospitality when they had not even met him before. MacCaig was habitually out all day and every day fishing. He would come home and put his feet in hot water in the evening. Isabel would cook fish and read Tolstoy. Ewen, his son, who often accompanied him, was also a keen fisherman.

MacCaig took Valerie and some of her friends on one occasion to the Culag Bar in Lochinver. He had a landrover which he borrowed when he was up there. Valerie later maintained that he drove all the way to the 'Culag' without looking once at the road!

Sea fishing is Lochinver's main industry. MacCaig wrote many poems[9] which have to do with the sea, the fish, the sea birds, the boat returning to Lochinver, and also poems set on the pier where he stood observing such mundane objects as fish boxes and winches, transforming them in his imagination until they became objects of fascination. In 'Lesson' the fishbox becomes a coffin for mackerel and this 'coffin' image creeps into the poet's nightmare and he imagines himself as a fish cramped in its tight confines.

He loved to describe the antics of the various types of sea birds, their ways of diving, flying and calling, and some of his finest poetry is in fact about them:[10]

> A gull slews in with icefloes in his eyes
> And a seal of crimson dapper on his beak;
> A frosty distance follows where he flies.
>
> Yet see him, pick-and-run, as he hauls a herring
> Through slats of a fishbox, ululating oaths
> In a sort of Eskimo at whatever stands
> Between his greed and his belly—see him swerving
> Out of infinity, steered by guts and glands.[11]

In some poems, the poet is perched up like an eagle on a rock[12] or lying like a lizard on sand dunes above the sea, looking at it from a distance, watching a wave unfolding itself along the bay. In other poems he is out in a boat hauling up crans of 'gleaming silver'. His boats have human qualities; he has a relationship with them, or they take on qualities of other objects; of one he says, 'In crossrips it's awkward as a piano'.[13]

On the pier at Lochinver stands the large and imposing Culag Hotel. The bar is separate from the hotel building and lies very near the quayside. It was originally called the Culag Bar but has now been renamed Scottie's Corner. MacCaig wrote several poems set in or just outside the bar, describing the people, sights and sounds.[14]

In the evenings the bar is jam-packed, especially in the summer. There are, in fact, two bars, known as the 'deep end' (where the locals go) and the 'shallow end' (where the tourists go). As the night wears on talk flows effortlessly on a lubricating stream of whisky. The bar becomes a fortress of light, warmth and colour to keep out the cold, briny, air outside, the restless sea and the wind. 'Fishermen's Pub':

> I leaned on the bar, not thinking, just noticing.
> I read the labels thumbed on the bright bottles.
> (To gallop on White Horse through Islay Mist!
>
> To sail into Talisker on Windjammer Rum!)
> Above my head the sick TV trembled
> And by the dartboard a guitar was thrumming
>
> Some out of place tune...Others have done this
> Before me. Remember, in one of the Russias,
> Alexander Blok drunk beyond his own mercy—

How he saw, through the smoke and the uproar,
His 'silken lady' come in and fire
The fire within him? I found myself staring

For mine, for that wild, miraculous presence
That would startle the world new with her forgivingness
But nothing was there but sidling smokewreaths

And through the babble all I heard was,
(Sounding, too near, in my dreadful silence)
A foreign guitar, the death clack of dominoes.

After the bar closed in the evening the various 'buddies' would leave and go to someone's house to continue their talk. Sometimes a group would drive up to Achmelvich to MacCaig's cottage.

MacCaig never did any writing during his annual visits to Assynt, preferring to spend his time walking, fishing and relaxing. He did not even keep a writer's notebook. As he once said, he was far too busy doing nothing!

He wrote the poem 'A man in Assynt' for a T.V. documentary. The narrative was then read against background shots of scenery, wild life etc., around Lochinver and Inverkirkaig. Some of MacCaig's friends in Lochinver like this poem best because it is so full of local allusions.

The poem, which is somewhat political, is in the form of a discussion. The poet keeps repeating the question 'Who owns this landscape?' followed by conjecture. He then explores his beloved landscape and gives us a series of sketches of it interspersed with rather sad sections pointing out how people have suffered as a result of their poor circumstances living there. The underlying tension of the poem rests on the fact that, at the time it was written, those who in fact owned the landscape and its true 'inheritors' were different. It was owned largely by Lord Vestey, an English businessman, but its 'people' were the poor crofters and fishermen who lived there. The poet asks, ironically, 'Whom does the sea belong to?'

He regrets that circumstances and poverty have led to depopulation. The poem, however, ends on an optimistic note, with the hope that 'the tide will turn' and that people will once again

> ...flood
> the bays and the sheltered glens
> with new generations replenishing the land
> with its richest of riches and coming, at last,
> into their own again.

In fact to a certain extent he got his wish because in 1992 the 21,000 acre Sutherland estate of North Lochinver[15] was put up for sale and a group of Sutherland crofters, who had formed themselves into a company called 'The Assynt Crofters'

Trust' bought it. This meant that the crofters owned all the sporting, fishing and mineral rights as well as the croft land itself.

Teaching
13. and Tutoring

In 1969 MacCaig, having finished his spell as Writer in Residence at Edinburgh University, became Headmaster at Inch Primary School in Liberton, Edinburgh. During this time he was invited out to dinner one evening by Professor Cotterill (who was then the Principal of Stirling University) and Professor Dunn, of the English Studies Department. They put to him the idea that he should go to Stirling University as a lecturer in English Studies. MacCaig had already in fact been two or three times to lecture there. While interested in the idea, he emphasised to them that his degree was in Classics and that all his experience was of teaching in Primary School. He also made one or two conditions. He said that he would not give lectures on pre-modern literature such as *Beowulf* and Jacobean Drama and that he would not go on committees. They agreed to these terms and so, in due course, he joined the staff.

The professors wished to appoint him because they recognised that it was a good thing in an English Department to have one person who was not a professional academic and whose approach to literature was different from the academics; they also thought it would be good to have a writer on the staff. The lecturers at Stirling felt that there should be a place for writers in residence. This was common practice in America but at that time it was very unusual in this country. MacCaig said of the appointment, 'At the back of their heads, I think, they were offering me an Eventide Home!'

The children at 'The Inch' bitterly resented the fact that he was leaving and they told him so. They dragged him up the stairs and said: 'Come up and see us and tell us why you are going to Stirling University!'

MacCaig worked at Stirling from 1970 to 1978. In 1972 he was given an additional designation, that of Reader in Poetry.

His work consisted mainly of taking tutorials and he offered seminars on modern Scottish literature, American poetry and contemporary European poetry in translation. He did the Scottish poets—Sydney Goodsir Smith, Edwin Morgan, Iain Crichton Smith, Alexander Scott; American poets—Ginsberg, Wallace Stevens, Robert Frost, Ferlinghetti and William Carlos Williams; Russian poets—Yevtushenko, Voznesenski; Tranströmer (Swedish), Herbert (Polish), Holub (Czech), Bertolt Brecht (German) and Montale (Italian). He showed a preference for East European poetry rather than the more lush and romantic writing of the Italian and Spanish poets. The East European poets tend to work in concrete images which translate with less loss of meaning than the more elaborate language of the 'romantics'. He was enthusiastic about twentieth century Russian poets. MacCaig had a dislike of the work of certain poets and tended to say so, as frequent references to 'Mr Ezra Inflated Pound' showed!

He was against the very detailed analysis of poetry often indulged in at universities, being more interested in poetry as art—as something to be enjoyed and savoured, rather than a piece of writing to be picked to bits and mangled by over-discussion.

Most of the teaching was done in small groups. There were very few examinations and a lot of emphasis was therefore put on continuous assessment. MacCaig, in discussing students' work with them, could be disapproving if he considered their work either went into too much fussy detail or alternatively if they went to the other extreme and wrote in a sketchy manner which did not contain much of substance. He was hard on them if they did not keep to what was in the text they were studying, having no time for vagueness. He hated the attempt some people make to relate their own inner conflicts to a poem even if in doing so they have to misinterpret it. He disliked students indulging in this 'emotional splurging' type of writing. In fact he was a person who shied away from emotional breast-beating in any way. He did not like cant, and had a hard cutting edge against these things in his dealings with students, or anybody else.

The staff had to write progress reports on the students. These were 'open', i.e. the students could read their own reports. MacCaig was a master of the epigrammatic progress report. He would characterise students. One read:

A mouse. Not just a mouse—a quiet mouse.

Another read:

She tries hard to be invisible. And usually succeeds.

He gave no lectures except for the occasional one on MacDiarmid. He was very reluctant to give lectures in fact. He felt it was not for him to stand up and pontificate on a subject, much preferring the informality of tutorials and seminars where there was more student involvement and he could talk in his normal conversational and throw-away style.

He did not have to be on committees, and he was never a 'committee man'. Nor did he radiate much excitement about attending Departmental meetings. He would usually start to fret after half an hour but was on the whole mild mannered and polite in his day to day dealings with colleagues.

On one occasion MacCaig was introduced to an academic psychologist who was interested in trying to track down people's creative urges, to encapsulate 'creativity' in some sort of theoretical butterfly net so that he could study it.

'What', he said to MacCaig, with a fixed look, 'is on your mind when you are writing a poem?'

MacCaig with students, about 1981
(photo: Jessie Ann Matthew)

This was exactly the sort of question that MacCaig hated and also the solemn approach that went with it. He quoted Satchmo: 'Man, I don't dig that kind of question!'

He was never an enthusiast for the more prosaic details of academic life and Alasdair Macrae, a colleague of MacCaig's at Stirling, recalled his technique for dealing with them:

> He found the finicky, pernickety, pedantic 'checking your footnotes' kind of quality tiresome. But if he got annoyed, he did not stand in the corridor and bawl and shout at people. He retreated. It was fun to watch his face when somebody was becoming tedious. His face was a study. He actually said almost nothing. He would say things to the point and he was extremely polite and patient with people with whom he did not get on. He tended not to remember their names![1]

At Stirling MacCaig was no longer billed as a 'Writer in Residence', so fewer people approached him with poetry. He did, however, still take an interest in helping any student who did creative writing and wanted help and criticism of his or her work. The keen ones would seek him out. And he was very patient and kind to them. In fact one or two started to write very 'MacCaigish' poems!

14. | Literary Life

On 7 May 1970, in Edinburgh, some people got together to set up a poetry reading and folk song group called 'The Heretics'. The chief instigators were Stuart MacGregor and William Neill. MacGregor was a lecturer and researcher with Edinburgh University Medical School and also wrote novels, poetry and folk songs. William Neill is a poet. Dolina MacLennan, the Gaelic singer, was also one of the founder members and organisers.

MacGregor and Neill thought that literary and artistic circles in Edinburgh were dominated by the Arts Council and certain magazines which were too much in favour of well-established writers and did not do enough to promote new talent; that they were out of touch with Scotland's cultural pulse. The aim of the Heretics was to act as a counter weight to this arts 'establishment'. They also had a strong Scottish Nationalist bias. Their purpose was to promote new authors, poets and musicians, and to give them a platform for reading and performing their work in public. The group gave the first start in poetry and prose reading to a number of writers, e.g. Roderick Watson, John Herdman, Donald Campbell and David Campbell; and various folk singers, including the Cruickshank sisters. MacCaig, who was a friend of MacGregor, and in fact taught him a lot about poetry, would suggest students whom MacGregor might invite to begin reading with the Heretics.

MacCaig appeared often with this group. He was one of their staple resources—one of the 'names' they used to draw people to their meetings. Another 'name' who appeared frequently was the poet, Robert Garioch. Garioch was a small, unassuming man—one could easily ignore him in a crowd. He was the 'ordinary little man at the back'. Yet his poems, when he read them, revealed a totally unsuspected mind in this homely exterior; a mind sparkling with wit, a man who watched his fellows closely and could see straight through the pompous official, the overbearing headmaster, the 'show-off' writer. He recorded in comic style some of the more ridiculous aspects of Edinburgh's pomp and circumstance, looking in particular at the Festival, the arts scene and occasions of civic dignity. His verses both mocked and celebrated the life and spectacle of Edinburgh. He wrote mainly in Scots. Like MacCaig, he was educated at the Royal High School and Edinburgh University. He became a teacher of English and latterly became Writer in Residence at Edinburgh University from 1971-72.

MacGregor and Neill only belonged to the Heretics for about two years. MacGregor was tragically killed in a car accident in Jamaica in 1973.

The Heretics meetings were informal and enjoyable affairs. The regular meetings were held in the basement bar at the New Town Hotel. Sydney Goodsir Smith once read at this hotel during a power cut. He was more or less blind in one eye and in the other he had a monocle. The cellar bar where the reading was taking place had a fake vaulted ceiling and the walls were decorated with implements and brass and candles. Goodsir Smith was reading a piece, ironically enough, about spring in the Botanic Gardens. The power was cut and people started lighting the candles. All one could see were eyes shining in the dark. Goodsir Smith tried to point his candle at the poem like a torch and wax went all over the poem. However, he managed to continue reading. It was as if the audience and poet had suddenly been transported back to 1780!

Another reader transported her audience even further back. In 1970 Ada Kay, the playwright, who believes she is a reincarnation of James IV, read an excerpt from her autobiography of the King, *Falcon*. Appearing in a black cloak, she asked for the lights to be lowered. She then gave a psychic history of James IV and of how she came to believe she was him. It was a wonderfully theatrical and histrionic perform-ance. She lived the whole thing and at one point she broke down and wept over some event in his life.

Heretics meetings were always unpredictable because of their policy of giving a platform to unknowns. Some of the poetry read aloud was of doubtful quality or so obscure in meaning that the audience would start to fall asleep over their half pints. On the other hand, some very talented writers did emerge. In addition to the writers there were a few regular singers like Dolina MacLennan, Morag Park, the Cruickshank sisters, Mary McGookin and Jimmie and Morag Dunbar.

At about this time, MacCaig met the Irish poet Seamus Heaney for the first time. Heaney recalls:

I first met Norman in February 1973, when my wife and I were travelling to a poetry festival in St Andrews. On our way through Edinburgh we had arranged to have coffee with him in a hotel—the North British, I think—and he then took us round for a dram and a bite of lunch in the Abbotsford, one of the great literary pubs of the age. There we had our grilled haddocks and were introduced to Gavin Muir, son of the poet Edwin Muir. I could hardly believe it was all happening. I also remember being instructed that the Glenmorangie whisky we were drinking was not pronounced (as I had long assumed) to rhyme with the Italian *piange* but with the English word—if it exists—orangey.[1]

MacCaig was to see a lot more of Heaney. In 1974 MacCaig went to Ireland with Sorley MacLean, for the launching in Dublin of the Claddagh recordings of their work. Paddy Moloney of the 'Chieftains',[2] who was involved in the management of Claddagh Records, was there as were the Irish poets, Heaney and John Montague. MacCaig and MacLean stayed in the Wicklow Mountains in a castle owned by

Garech de Brun, whose mother belonged to the Guinness family. It was while they were staying the night at the castle that MacCaig later maintained that MacLean fell asleep in the middle of one of his own sentences!

Heaney, who was also at the castle on this occasion, has described—using fishing metaphors—MacCaig's techniques for provocation during a session round the table:

> He was a great fisherman, a master of the cast, of the line that is a lure…One night in Garech de Brun's home in Co. Wicklow, after an evening at the Abbey Theatre to launch *The Way I Say It*, a record of Norman reading his poems, he was working the table as merrily and deliberately as he would have worked a salmon pool. And next thing, he landed a perfectly baited line in front of me, like a little test, just to see how I'd jump.
>
> 'I can't stand,' he said—the first flex of the rod—'I can't stand gloomy, ambitious poetry.' Meaning, from another angle, 'This is just a wee jag because of the dark and earnest mood of your bog poems.' (These were being published here and there at the time). Meaning, from yet another angle, 'Robert Lowell's poetry is overrated and you should beware of being influenced by him.' (Not that I was, then).
>
> I don't know what imp inspired me, but I remember that I managed to leap free and flick back with, 'So I suppose Robert Herrick[3] is the one for you, Norman.' Cheeky, but called for. I date our real friendship from that moment.[4]

During the course of their Dublin trip, MacCaig and Sorley MacLean gave a talk on television. They were elaborately made up before they went on. MacCaig was used to being made up to go on T.V., but this was far more intensive make up than anything he had ever experienced. When they were ready to appear, MacCaig said to the others, of himself, 'A terrible beauty is born'!

MacCaig in fact went to Ireland on several occasions—to Dublin, Belfast and Kilkenny and to the new University of Coleraine.

Sorley MacLean has described himself and MacCaig as 'opposites' as regards the subjects they write about, MacCaig tending, as he says, to be a 'miniaturist', MacLean using a much wider canvas and more sweeping 'brush strokes'. MacLean's poetry has a broad, slow, sweeping, elemental quality—MacCaig's is angular, jocular, rapid and witty. There is much more overt emotion in MacLean's poetry. He uses his own experiences and the history of his people. MacLean is one of the great oral historians of the Western Islands. In conversation he can talk for hours about the way the Highlanders have been ruthlessly exploited over the past 200 years and can trace the individual involvement of families in historical events.

While MacCaig's poetry was based often on his own experiences, he was more reticent than MacLean, much less 'romantic' and less emotional. While MacLean uses big features—the mountains and the sea—in MacCaig's poems these are often the background to something on a smaller scale, for example a flock of gulls or an individual fishing boat or himself.

Despite MacLean's dislike of MacCaig's early poetry, they latterly became friends.

MacCaig in fact was one of the first scholars who spoke with enthusiasm and knowledge of the poetry of MacLean in years when MacLean's work, written in Gaelic with English translations, tended to be neglected by English speakers.

Back in Edinburgh, towards the end of the 1960s, Bob Watt, hero of Milne's Bar, raconteur and barman, retired. As Alan Bold said, sadly: '...that of course was that: the ba' was well and truly burst.'[5] In 1971 George Mackay Brown, returning briefly to Edinburgh, described a visit to Milne's Bar:

> The old familiar tavern in Rose Street is full of new faces—yes, and the old beery tables have been removed and oak beams put across the dark smoky ceiling, and the place is full of young barmaids (all the faithful old retainers, except one, are gone). What still remains are the photographs of Scotland's poets—a gey mixture—along the walls. So, among all these strangers, I sigh and down my pint of export, and grasp my single piece of baggage, and wait for the bus in the cold darkening air outside...[6]

But the poetry vogue continued. In addition to Heretics readings, there was considerable poetry reading activity too at this time at Edinburgh University. On Saturday, 26 February 1972, in the David Hume Tower at the University, an event was held called 'Poem 72'—an all day festival of poetry, mostly Scottish. Among the well-known poets who read were MacCaig, Edwin Morgan and Robert Garioch. But it was also used as a platform for talented younger poets like Liz Lochhead and for unknown poets who were thought to deserve a hearing. About 1,000 people came to this, despite a power cut from noon till 3 p.m.! Describing the party held in his flat for the poets, including MacCaig and others, after this event, one of the organisers, John Schofield, wrote:

> Around midnight. At my flat, the celebration is in full swing. Outside are three carloads of policemen, silent, watching. I wonder what a stimulating experience it would be to share a night in jail with Scotland's literary cream, researching, as Duncan Glen once suggested, into vocabulary changes and alcohol in the bloodstream. Luckily they are bursting somebody else's party. I ask Garioch to inscribe a *Selected Poems* for me, and he signs it Rumboat Beerioch. One of my stewardesses floats up to me and sighs, 'Have you ever danced with Norman MacCaig?'[7]

MacCaig loved dancing at student and Heretics parties. He would take part whatever dance it was. He would learn in a moment all the rhythms and all the steps and gestures and he would also make mock of them at the same time as dancing them. There was a showman side to MacCaig: a joker, an extrovert, who appeared at parties and after one or two whiskies. Another favourite occupation of his at these parties was to argue. Being an adept at polemics, he would get someone to make a statement of his ideas, then repeat to him what he had just said and ask him to confirm that that was the gist of his argument. People invariably agreed with this—not noticing that he had given the argument a small twist. He would then get hold of the small twist he had given it and proceed to argue against his contender who would eventually find that he was arguing about something quite other than the original idea he had put forward!

On 27 May 1972, to mark the forthcoming eightieth birthday of Hugh MacDiarmid, a gathering of academics and others spent the day at Edinburgh University discussing his poetry and its place in Scottish life and letters. MacDiarmid was present at this as were MacCaig, Sydney Goodsir Smith and Sorley MacLean. A poetry reading evening was organised at the Reid School of Music in Edinburgh on 5 September, again to celebrate MacDiarmid's birthday. David Leigh, reporting on this in the *Scotsman* of the next day, wrote:

> Last night was a tribal celebration, from the essence of which a Sassenach would be excluded. The magazine *Scottish International*, a focus for the younger and more radical intellectual nationalists, mounted the occasion.
>
> Norman MacCaig, Robert Garioch and Sorley MacLean—major Scottish middle-aged poets writing respectively in English, both English and Scots, and Gaelic—acted as warm-up men. The Scottish Arts Council contributed a 35-minute documentary film they have commissioned on the man. And the 300-seat hall was packed. Tonight the poet will appear again, with the Heretics in Charlotte Street.
>
> This necklace of admiration was placed round the sturdy throat of Hugh MacDiarmid, who is 80 years old. He was just a little unsteady as he mounted the platform, but read his poetry erect and pugnacious as befits his status. Much of MacDiarmid's greatness lies in his refusal ever to see his energies diverted, or suffocated, or thwarted, and the energy seems—miraculously—not to evaporate as his body ages. His 90th birthday seems likely to be quite an event—and even his 100th.

By this time MacDiarmid was a small, frail, figure. He was usually accompanied at these events by his wife, Valda.

MacCaig wrote several poems about or for MacDiarmid. In 'A writer' he paid tribute to his friend's ability to withstand the slings and arrows of life.

In January, 1975, Sydney Goodsir Smith, great friend of MacCaig and fellow writer, died. Stanley Roger Green wrote:

> S.G.S. was a man of many paradoxes and apparent contradictions, and definition was not easy. A gentlemanly product of Establishment forcing-houses yet a dedicated Scottish Nationalist; a life-long socialist with aristocratic tastes; a romantic lyricist who could employ the forensic argumentative skill of a Q.C.; and in company, a rumbustious Falstaffian whose genial gaiety enlivened all who knew him, yet in private a person profoundly distressed by man's inhumanity.[8]

The Heretics continued to function both in Edinburgh and in small theatres and arts centres all round the country. Just about every notable poet in Scotland took part in these readings at some time or another.

One poet who began to appear often in the late 1970s with them was Liz Lochhead, then an art teacher from Glasgow. She writes rather biting, humorous poetry, often about women. She has since become well known as a playwright. John Herdman, the writer, who in the early 1970s was the Secretary of the Heretics, was usually at the meetings and occasionally read excerpts from his own novels, noted for their black humour. Adam MacNaughtan, then a Glasgow school teacher, also appeared on many occasions, singing and reciting humorous songs and poems. He has an exceptionally resonant voice and gave the key words extra spice by barking them out as he sang them. MacCaig featured often on their programme, and was an influential figure, as Michael Aitken noted:

Norman has done much to revitalise the reading of poetry in Scotland. Douglas Eadie once described him as the Henry Cooper of the poetry scene—getting on a bit but still with the wickedest left-hook in the business. Only at a reading does one fully appreciate the sense of the comic in his work; the man can be quite extraordinarily funny.[9]

If he was reading, he usually topped the bill except on the rare occasions when MacDiarmid appeared. On one occasion, in 1974, they appeared at the same reading.[10] MacDiarmid was helped on to the platform by MacCaig who, in his friend's latter years, acted as a sort of batman to him, helping him off and on stages and escorting him in and out of recital halls. A literary friend referred to them as 'Don Quixote and Sancho Panza'. MacDiarmid was clutching an enormous briefcase. He sank down into a chair beside a little table and slowly and deliberately produced book after book from the case, piling them up on the table while the audience looked on in total silence. He then took one book and started to hunt for a poem. The silence deepened; all that could be heard was the sound of one page after another flicking over! After what seemed like forever, he found what he wanted, cleared his throat and set off.

He read several poems, including 'Old Wife in High Spirits' and 'Crowdieknowe'. He had a curious voice; cultured, almost genteel in its intonation and yet at the same time vibrant. There was nothing genteel about the poems however. They were as sentimental as a bomb raid. MacDiarmid delighted in using poetry as a vehicle for violent pronouncements, passionate outpourings, denunciations, powerful evocations. In 'Old Wife in High Spirits' he advocated the virtues of whisky for old women. His old lady, enlivened by the barley bree, had a high time of it socialising in the pub—not for her the safe cautious preservation of energy and resources so often seen in elderly people. After a few drinks every ancient muscle and artery and brain cell was throbbing and hopping with life:

Ninety per cent o' respectable folk never hae
As muckle life in their creeshy carcases frae beginnin' to end
As kythed in that wild auld carline that day!

MacCaig was very fond of MacDiarmid. He was very moved by the man's courage, dignity and achievements. They had a jocular relationship. Latterly MacDiarmid was very deaf and MacCaig became his interpreter. If they were appearing at the same reading MacCaig would play with the audience at MacDiarmid's expense. The old man just sat there holding his ear and smiling over his pipe.

15. Later Poems

After a gap of four years, two books of poems were published in fairly quick succession, *The White Bird* in 1973, and *The World's Room* in 1974.

More thoughts about old age were creeping in. In 'Old crofter' the man is losing his grip; gates fall off hinges, the haycocks he builds are lopsided, he does not secure his boat properly. In 'Old man' the man is living in the past—the present holds no 'nourishment' for him.

Feelings of compassion are more evident in the poems than formerly. In 'Milne's Bar' MacCaig is the kind friend listening to another's troubles.

There is also in some poems a feeling of moving into a minor key. 'Reversal' shows his dislike of those who, for reasons of popularity and profit, attempt to 'tame' the wild. They paint stones and sell them, brighten up sad melodies, simplify them and in the end kill them. He had a love of the mournful, complex pibroch tune and hated to hear its 'domesticated' form.

Seamus Heaney noted this in MacCaig once:

One day at a party in Edinburgh, in a room full of smoke and music and flirtation, Norman took me into a corner and began to whistle a totally bewitching air. It was a fragment of *pibroch*, a few orphaned phrases as piercing as a curlew-call, but it was also a melody of the soul's loneliness, a tune that was like a piece of secret knowledge. It has grown stronger and clearer in my memory and nowadays I link it with the clarity of conscience and the moral strength that impelled and sustained MacCaig in the course of his protest as a conscientious objector during the Second World War. I link it also with his labyrinthine ironies and courtesies, the way in which he maintained a debonair style and yet kept faith with a history of loss.[1]

In 'Greenshank' MacCaig evokes the sad calling of this bird, describes it and its habits in detail and then makes a startling parallel of the bird and his own 'melancholy':

> He is the melancholy that flies
> in the weathers of my mind,

> He is the loneliness that calls to me there
> in a semitone
> of desolate octaves.

The poem, which starts off as a poem about the call of a bird, becomes a poem about a state of mind.

Erik Frykman has pointed to 'the numerous poems in which a graphic description of physical scenery is followed by an observation on the poet's self.'[2] Probably this was one of MacCaig's most commonly used devices and was evident throughout his life as a poet. For instance, in 'A good day' (*WB*, not in *CP*) he compares his own stance in life to that of the heron standing on a steeply shelving dangerous bank—a metaphor, perhaps, for the dangerous depths of his own thoughts into which he does not wish to venture too far.

Another trait in MacCaig which occasionally surfaced in his later poems was his 'home bird' tendency, already mentioned in an earlier chapter. He admitted to being rather ashamed of the fact that he had never been involved in 'life' to the extent of struggling along with the oppressed; those involved in famine or unrest. There was a streak in him of non-involvement. He was not a 'fighter to right the wrongs of society' but more of an observer. He, however, had no such feelings about his pacifist stance during the Second World War. He had no intention of ever fighting and killing others for the sake of anyone. But he had within himself a feeling of unease at times at the fact that he had been so lucky in life as to be spared some of the horrors that afflict others.

Several poems bring out these feelings, 'Home bird' (*MP*, not in *CP*) particularly, and 'Convicted' (*TS*, not in *CP*). He said of these:

> The poem 'Home bird' is about me. It is the personification of the happiness that is inside me. She that is inside me. It is an aspect of myself that I am a home bird. I have been a happy chap all my days. This is about this inbuilt instinct towards being a happy fellow. The relations again are personifications, not particular people. The 'cousin smelling of smoke' stands for news of places such as Ulster. These thoughts shake my natural happiness.
>
> 'Convicted' is about much the same thing. It is about me sitting here and not being involved in those dreadful things happening elsewhere and sometimes one feels guilty. I stay here locked in the prison of myself. I like to concretise abstract thought.[3]

He continued in this vein in 'Behind a shut door' (*WB*, not in *CP*) where he writes about some of the sad and tragic things in life—a refugee, a caged bird and a lonely, crying child and his own lack of concern for them:

> I take no heed
> A crime that every day I commit
> And hate and hate myself because of it.

*MacCaig at the Leamington Lift Bridge, on the Union Canal
near his home in Edinburgh* (photo: Jessie Ann Matthew)

A later example is 'Found guilty'. Here he watches a baby sandpiper flying over water, then flying lower and lower, and then trying to fly in the water and drowning, and he uses this as a metaphor for friends whom he has watched having a bad time while he has stood by without helping. This 'confessional' type of poetry is very much a later development and has a rather Donne-like touch to it.

In *The World's Room* (1974), we find a more contemplative vein of poetry, seen in such poems as 'The Pass of the Roaring' and the nostalgic 'Return to Scalpay'. In about 1970 (when aged 60) MacCaig went on a return visit to this island with an artist friend, Hamish Lawrie. In this poem he reverts from free verse to a more formal style of writing. Evoking his childhood memories and comparing them with his feelings on returning so many years later, he writes in a fairly simple style. There is a tremendous feeling of nostalgia here—a tugging at the heartstrings:

> My city eyeballs prickle; it's hard to bear
> With such affection and such gaiety.

MacCaig, older, wiser, more tolerant, is flooded by feelings of defencelessness against the sheer kindness and goodness of these people.

The last two stanzas contain a character sketch of his cousin Johann, a large, lovable woman—an emotional person who could be laughing one moment, crying the next—'easy glum, easy glow' as a friend would say of her. In this poem 'artist' MacCaig sketches her figure 'monumental against the flying sky'. She has all the solidity of a figure in a primitive painting.

'Below the Clisham, Isle of Harris: after many years', brings out the Gaelic side of MacCaig: his sense of belonging to Harris and the Hebrides; the immensity of the natural elements and the minuteness of an old woman and her cow. She accepts MacCaig, makes him feel at home. She is symbolic of her people's history—seems to link past and present. She epitomises the easy, undemanding friendliness of the Gael; the dependence of humans on one another in this land where the elements dominate life and all human contact is treasured and friendships are very important. It is a rather sombre poem.

This tendency to look back continues in 'Drop-out in Edinburgh'. The poem is similar in imagery to 'In my mind'. In both of them the poet is walking about Edinburgh, recalling the past. The city to him is a hundred memories, a hundred images, rather like something seen in a kaleidoscope. 'Drop-out in Edinburgh' is written in a surreal mood—reminiscent of Wallace Stevens. It is about the city and yet it does not describe it. Here the poet has a very personal relationship with his home town. The phrase 'I am your incandescent heir' is repeated twice, as the second line of the poem and at the beginning of the final section. In between lies a long section about the city. It is written in a trance-like way, with long sentences running over several lines and strange ideas and images piled one on the other:

> City of everywhere, broken necklace in the sun,
> you are caves of guilt, you are pinnacles of jubilation.

Your music is a filigree of drumming.
You frown into the advent of heavenly hosts.
　　…When the sea
breathes gray over you, you become
one lurking-place, one shifting of nowheres—
in it are warpipes and genteel pianos
and the sawing voices of lawyers.

In his 1976 article for *Chapman,* 'My Way of It', he described, among other things, how he wrote poetry:

When I feel like writing a poem, I sit down with a blank sheet of paper and no idea whatever in my head. Into it, where there's plenty of room, enters the memory of a place, an emotional experience, a person, or, most commonly, a phrase, and the poem stalactites down the page from that. This means I'm into the poem, various distances, before I know what it's about. In fact I don't know what the whole poem's about till I've finished it. This sounds daft, but I believe it's a common enough experience with poets...

Many poets polish and refine and eliminate and add, making version after version of the original attempt. I can't do that. The poem, whatever it's worth, generally comes easily and quickly and pretty often with no correction at all, and once it's on the page, that's that. This hit or miss way of writing means that I write a lot. It also means I write a lot of unimprovable duds. I reckon at least half, probably more, of what I write I put in the bucket—an act I relish almost as much as writing the things. It's a wasteful form of production which I recommend to nobody.

My notions about the value of poetry and the ways it is produced are, I've come to notice, fairly low-falutin'. I never met a White Goddess in my life and when I find myself in the company of singing robes, hieratic gestures and fluting voices I phone a taxi. The pleasure in making a poem lies in making them and seems to me not different from a true craftsman's pleasure in making a table, or a meal to put on it, or a boat that marries the water as a boat should. The pleasure in making something that was never in the world before, with our gifts and abilities at their farthest stretch, is surely one that is common to everybody.

The total opposite to MacCaig is Yeats who was the most laborious writer, producing version after version of every poem he ever wrote.

This 'low-falutin' attitude to poetry came across in a radio interview in 1993 (some years after Isabel's death). Edi Stark, the interviewer, caught him in facetious mood:

Stark: How did Isabel feel about you writing poetry?
MacCaig: She thought I was a poet. Poor thing! After all she only had a first class honours in English, she could hardly know!

Stark: She encouraged you?

MacCaig: Not voluntarily.

Stark: How did you feel about her being your muse?

MacCaig: We didn't talk like that.

Stark: Did she ever pick up your poems and say 'this is absolutely brilliant'!

MacCaig: She would know better than to speak like that to me! She would say 'not bad'. After six months I would pick out the best and show them to her.

Stark: She did not have a sneaky wee look?

MacCaig: Her? Never!

Stark: She must have seen them in the early days.[4]

MacCaig: Oh, I suppose so.[5]

There is no doubt, however, that Isabel took a great interest in the poems and that she is the anonymous central figure in quite a few of them.

16. Old Friends

> Language thou art too narrow, and too weak
> To ease us now; great sorrow cannot speak...
> *John Donne*[1]

When MacCaig was travelling to poetry readings in the north in January, 1976, he was contacted by Mrs A.K. MacLeod. She asked him to visit MacLeod who was suffering ill health and had been for a spell in hospital. Although he had got home, Mrs MacLeod knew that his health was deteriorating. MacCaig went to Inverkirkaig to stay with them. One evening A.K., unlike his usual self, said that he would go to bed early. In the morning he woke feeling very ill and spitting up blood. MacCaig and Mrs MacLeod were with him and just before he died his last word was 'Norman'.

MacCaig, speaking about him later in a radio interview, said:

And they [friends] are terribly important to me. And one in particular, a man called Angus MacLeod. When he died the locals would say things like, 'Oh he was a clever boy, you know, he could have been the manager of the Bank of England', because in material things he was a total failure, but he wasn't a failure at all—he never did a thing he didn't want to do and he gave more pleasure to more people, including me, than anybody.[2]

In the book *The Equal Skies* (published 1980), he wrote a whole series of 'Poems for Angus'. They describe travelling to his friend's house to see him, his death, funeral, grief, poems in his praise and a poem about his dog. These poems, which appear at the start of *The Equal Skies*, set the tone for a more sombre book than in the past. Between 1975 and 1978 MacCaig in fact lost six of his closest friends and this affected him deeply.

The poems to Angus are written in a beautifully spare, honed-down style—there is nothing fancy or elaborate in them. They are simple, understated and yet have a tug of authentic grief.[3] As MacCaig implies in the poems, if one feels terrible grief for a departed friend that in a way is a celebration of the friendship—it proves what a close friendship it was.

> We laugh and we sing, but we all know we're thinking
> Of the one who isn't here.
>
> The laughter and the singing are paper flowers
> laid on a wet grave in an empty darkness.
> For we all know we're thinking
> of the one who can't be here,
> not even as a ghost smiling through the black window.[4]

MacCaig's atheism comes out in these poems:

> For a boat has sailed into
> the sea of unknowing;
> you are on board.
>
> And somewhere another boat
> rocks
> by another pier.
>
> It's waiting to take me
> where I'll never know you again—
> a voyage
> beyond knowledge, beyond memory.[5]

Shortly after MacLeod died, it was decided to renovate the house at Achmelvich where the MacCaigs used to live in the summer and so it was not made available for let that year. They then rented a house belonging to a friend, Norman MacAskill, at Inverkirkaig. This house is set high up on a shoulder of the hill looking out over the bay and the rocky coastline. It is an old croft house with a built-out porch at the entrance.

Meantime another ageing friend of MacCaig was approaching his 85th year. On Saturday, 13 August 1977, a concert was organised in the Assembly Rooms, Edinburgh, by the S.T.U.C. to honour the 85th birthday of MacDiarmid. At this, his literary friends paid tribute to him. The hall was draped with red banners and there was more than a hint of Marxism in the air. A bomb threat from an anonymous telephone caller further enlivened the proceedings. MacDiarmid, a small frail figure, sat in the front row beside his wife, Valda. At the end of the concert the old man was coaxed onto the stage. Julie Davidson described the scene:

> They trundled him on at the end of the evening, a tiny, shrivelled, stumbling figure, the monster captive, the toothless (perhaps) old lion there to be lionised. Jimmy Milne, the secretary of the Scottish TUC, held his hand as if he were a child or a tamed beast and said nervously: 'I don't know if he'll talk...he's very tired...I don't know if he'll say anything...' Whereupon the old lion opened his

mouth and roared.

All the teeth were in place. And what he roared was as uncompromising and impenitent as the rest of his life. At age 85, Hugh MacDiarmid is still demanding 'the rejection of the Monarchy and all it stands for, the break-up of Britain and the building of a Scottish Republic.'

The audience roared back. Socialists and Nationalists and perhaps even the apolitical, some kind of shared emotion kindled by the undiminished fire of the warrior bard.[6]

A year later he was dead. He was buried at Langholm cemetery on 13 September, 1978—a day of mist and fine rain. Many friends were present at the funeral: poets, artists, communists, actors, relatives, colleagues. MacCaig delivered a funeral oration over the coffin referring to MacDiarmid's ability by his sometimes explosive harshness to open the eyes of people who were 'blind' to their own abilities and potential. He ended:

This is a time for public goodbyes and greetings. I, for one, will be saying my private goodbyes and greetings to him for as long as I live.[7]

Then the piper, Seaumas MacNeil, played the 'Lament for the Children', a pibroch MacDiarmid had loved. The coffin was lowered into the grave and Valda, MacDiarmid's widow, scattered a bunch of small white roses on the coffin, which action recalled one of her husband's shortest and best-known poems:

> The rose of all the world is not for me.
> I want for my part
> Only the little white rose of Scotland
> That smells sharp and sweet—and breaks the heart.[8]

17. | Among the Media Men

In 1978 MacCaig retired from Stirling University. To mark the occasion, the University prepared a volume[1] of articles, poems and music which they gifted to him. In this Alasdair Macrae, one of the lecturers in the English Studies Department, wrote a short essay about MacCaig. The reference in it to the 'Marchmont rose' concerns a strange and rather inexplicable incident which involved the poet one night. MacCaig wrote about it himself in 'Midnight encounter'. Alasdair Macrae describes it:

Midnight. Norman ruminating homeward through the streets of Marchmont.[2] Stopped, attention arrested by a red rose in a scuffed patch against the houses. Door opened and man with scissors emerged. Snipped and presented the flower to Norman. No words. Door shut behind him.

Norman MacCaig does not suffer clever people gladly. He enjoys the enjoyment of others, whether in knowledge or music or people or things. His poetry is celebratory, whether the subject be a stonechat, a thorn bush or his late friend, A.K. MacLeod. In the years I have known him he has never imposed a grumble (although he has, on occasions, pressed a Grouse), never ground his opinions, never asked for my sympathy, pity or forbearance. His hospitable acceptance of battered friends and strayed strangers would make the Samaritan feel stingy.

When he leaves Stirling we shall find the regulation-width corridors that much narrower, we shall remember his leaven in the academic dough, we shall miss his high, laughing head at the bar. We shall come to appreciate his poetry more wisely; while he was here we could afford, we thought, to take his poems for granted, as subsumed in his presence. He has shared that Marchmont rose with all of us.

In March, 1977, the Scottish Arts Council produced a documentary film about MacCaig. Julie Davidson wrote about this:

When Norman MacCaig delivers his precise and tailored intimacies to an audience—and in spite of all he says to the contrary he is the arch performer among poets—he is readily able to persuade us that the loose use of language does serious damage to the world and its peoples.

He does no damage at all in his statement about himself and his work for the Scottish Arts Council, except to contradict himself once or twice (like most Gaels he is irresistibly attracted to the challenge of playing his own devil's advocate), and you can forgive him that for the riveting nature of his rhetoric.

'Norman MacCaig: A Man in My Position' is the sixth in a series of films about contemporary Scottish writers commissioned by the Arts Council, who have already done the right thing by Neil Gunn, Hugh MacDiarmid, Sorley MacLean and Eric Linklater. This one was made by Pelicula Films of Glasgow (in association with the Films of Scotland Committee) and the director, Mike Alexander, and cameraman, Mark Littlewood, have done the right thing by Norman MacCaig.

They have filmed him quietly, with restraint, in close communion with the contained quality of his language, adding no visual frills to its dense formality, displaying its richness against two simple backgrounds: the landscape of Assynt in Sutherland and the austere but mischievous face of MacCaig himself.

It was said that, during the making of the film, the poet refused to walk from point A to point B on the grounds that he was 'not an actor'. Of course he is an actor, and it was an actor's instinct that insisted his words, and not his postures, should be filmed (quite right) and that they should be delivered with astonishing virtuosity: the timing, the sudden rushes of images, the dramatic dragging of certain vowels and the faint sibilance make him an oracular snake mesmerising the audience and mocking himself.

He effortlessly upstages Magnus Magnusson, attempting to mine the master's mind with earnest schoolboy diggings into 'inspiration' and 'the real Norman MacCaig', and he manages, somehow, to dictate the tone of Mark Littlewood's clever camerawork on the Assynt landscape, which is invested with the classical formality of MacCaig's own Gaelic mode.

MacCaig has invented a motto for himself: 'Excess is not enough.' This film strikes an admirable balance between excessively indulging him and not giving us enough of him.[3]

MacCaig was later asked for his opinion of the film and said, smiling—'It exhausts the subject'. The film won a diploma of merit from the Melbourne Film Festival.

He was becoming famous, not only in Scotland but worldwide. As mentioned earlier, in 1977 a Swede, Erik Frykman, produced a work called *Unemphatic Marvels: A Study of Norman MacCaig's Poetry*.[4] In this he examined MacCaig's main themes and the patterns in his imagery, and made a brief critical assessment of some of the poems. Derek Bowman, reviewing the book, wrote:

This is genuine pioneering work on Mr Frykman's part, introducing to his fellow Swedes an important contemporary poet, while he is alive and at the height of his powers, thereby promoting that traffic of ideas, of shared experience which is bound to enrich the lives of many.[5]

From 1974 onwards MacCaig would appear to have fallen under the gentle but infinitely powerful influence of children, particularly perhaps his own grandchildren, Catherine and Frances, the daughters of Joan. Images from fairy tales appear. 'Woodsman' is a rather nasty fairy tale—a mysterious poem, rather like 'Hansel and Gretel' in its depiction of a woodsman and a wicked witch. There are one or two of these poems in other volumes, e.g. the much earlier poem 'Escapist' (1966) which describes a traveller in dark woods, a man with an axe and a howling wolf. The later 'Summer evening in Assynt' shows the village of Elphin in a 'green' light and evokes memories of Celtic legend and a frog and a princess.

There are also some poems about small children. 'Two-year-old' concerns his grand-daughter, Catherine. Like her grandfather, she exhibits an ability to 'see' other possibilities in the ordinary:

> She strokes a bottlebrush of clear water
> around the sink and says, *Red*.
>
> She dips the brush in the milk bottle
> and strokes again and says, *Yellow*.
> How carefully, how busily
> she paints the sink with clear water.

Another two-year-old threw himself sturdily into MacCaig's path. Christopher, Roderick Watson's[6] son, appears in 'Wooden chair with arms'. Again the child is in his own world of make-believe. He climbs the 'mountain' of the chair and laughs and jumps from it, showing off to MacCaig, who is sipping whisky and watching.

In March, 1980, in a BBC Radio Schools programme in the 'Chapbook' series, MacCaig presented a programme of poetry for 12 to 14 year olds, called 'Animals in Poetry', and in February, 1981, another in the same series called 'Writing of the Sea'.

He wrote one or two special poems for these. He was even known to write poetry for children 'on demand'! He corresponded regularly with his grand-daughters, Catherine and Frances, when they were small. They did not approve of the fact that he always smoked a great deal. One of the letters asked him to stop smoking and said that if he did not, he had to pay them a penalty by sending them a poem each!

'Jumping toad' is an example of a poem possibly written with children in mind. The poem is very visual and concerns a toad which looks grandmotherly but suddenly and outrageously flips out its tongue and swallows an ant. 'Toad' was also written about this time. MacCaig read it often at poetry readings. Before reading it, he always told the story or myth about the toad—that it is supposed to have a jewel in its head. 'Obvious nonsense', he concluded, 'There would be no toads left!' The poem has a vivid directness about it. He is talking to a toad which visited him in his cottage in Achmelvich and used to crawl under the door into the lobby, as if seeking human companionship.[7] It is likened to a Japanese wrestler in its curious crawling walk, its obesity. The poet gently carries the creature outside and sets it down under the stars and then, inspired by a correlation of images, says,

A jewel in your head? Toad,
you've put one in mine,
a tiny radiance in a dark place.

Ishbel MacLean, Sorley MacLean's daughter, was the producer of several radio programmes in which MacCaig featured, including the two just mentioned. She was a friend of his, having first met him when she was a student at Edinburgh University and he was Writer in Residence. She got on well with him because they liked to argue or spar with each other.

During one recording session at the BBC Ishbel and MacCaig were in different rooms and could hear but not see one another. He was muttering away and Ishbel, not satisfied with the sound, asked him to do something again. His lugubrious, drawling voice came through saying (of Ishbel),

'She could have been a warder in Belsen.'

Ishbel put her finger down on the 'talk back' button and said,

'I heard that!'

He replied,

'You were supposed to!'

In 1981 the Third Eye Centre in Glasgow held an Exhibition called 'Seven Poets' and this later toured the United Kingdom. They also published a book[8] in connection with this Exhibition which contains pictures, photographs and articles about the six major Scottish poets living at this time, namely, MacCaig, Iain Crichton Smith, George Mackay Brown, Robert Garioch, Sorley MacLean and Edwin Morgan. The seventh poet about whom some material was also included was, of course, Hugh MacDiarmid.

The pictures by Alexander Moffat caused a stir—some liked them and some didn't and in typical Scottish fashion said so in the magazines and newspapers of the land. Moffat's style of painting is influenced by Kitaj. The pictures have strong lines and all the poets appear as rather severe characters. There is a sort of 'Nordic gloom' about them. They are also reminiscent of Munch. He certainly does not flatter them, but he does seem, in a few lines, to catch something of the inner energy and sensitivity of each poet.

In one picture in particular, 'Poets' Pub' he has shown us all seven of them with, in addition, Sydney Goodsir Smith and Alan Bold, sitting in a pub. The central trio talking are MacDiarmid, Goodsir Smith and Mackay Brown and the other poets are grouped around them. The poets have a sort of fixed 'fly in amber' look about them. An article appeared in *The Scots Magazine* which was a profile of Robert Garioch by Marjorie Wilson. In this she wrote:

Alexander Moffat's composite portrait group of nine famous contemporary Scottish poets is a rogue's gallery indeed. Garioch himself thought they were a sinister-looking bunch, but denied that he had been purposely depicted as being rather aloof and withdrawn from the others. 'No, no. The figures were arranged like that for the sake of the composition. I'm not withdrawn at all really and I like meeting people.'[9]

On 3 June 1982, MacCaig was interviewed by Alastair Moffat for 'Encore' on S.T.V. Moffat showed him in three venues—in his home, at a poetry reading and in a pub. The conversation during the interview flowed effortlessly, full of humour and MacCaig's peculiar brand of sense/nonsense. It provided some insight into poetry as an art or craft with frequent forays into such side issues as the debunking of politicians.

MacCaig with interviewers tended to react like a glitter-ball, one of those revolving orbs covered in mirrors that sometimes hang above a dance floor. As it revolves it throws off lights, coloured according to the colour of the light thrown on it from outside. Interviewed by Moffat, who is a kindly, genuine, easy-going, relaxing fellow, we now saw reflected back a sharp, incisive MacCaig, the deep-set hooded eyes alternately being thoughtful or occasionally doing a peculiarly MacCaigian trick of suddenly looking off sideways as if trying to see round a corner and then coming back as if from some far off journey with the answer to a question. This happened particularly in the pub scene. It seems that to get MacCaig at his most wild, bizarre and fluent it was necessary to set him down in an atmosphere of button back seats, frosted glass mirrors, background chatter, the ringing telephone and general gentle uproar of a crowded Edinburgh pub.

MacCaig interviewed by a different interviewer appeared different. If one felt that he and the interviewer were not seeing eye to eye then the revolving orb reflected flashes of blue, little crackles of lightning in the form of disagreements, questions challenged, deliberately misleading statements or obscure comments made to trip up the interviewer, and short, rather cut-off replies. Some interviewers found this heavy going. 'I've never thought that Norman MacCaig…would be an easy subject for the lily-livered interviewer' as the writer O.K. Harris once said of him.[10] But even then a fairly aggressive interview could reveal a side of him which was interesting because there was a side to him which was aggressive and loved to argue—a side which revealed itself when he was up against disagreement or incomprehension.

MacCaig spoke best in conversation rather than when on his own making a formal speech or lecture. He was at his best talking in a situation where he was reacting to an interviewer or parrying jests with an audience, but when he did not have another person to strike sparks off, his talk could lose some of its sparkle. If one heard him doing a talk on the radio on his own, illustrated by readings, the effect was flatter than if one heard him talking and reading the poems to an audience.

The audience for the S.T.V. 'Encore' show was one at a Heretics poetry reading in Edinburgh. MacCaig was flanked by Liz Lochhead and Adam MacNaughtan, their faces reflecting what they thought of the poems. To one poem in particular, 'John Brown and Queen Victoria'—a spicy, barbed little piece making fun of Queen Victoria's brittle temperament and John Brown's difficulties in coping with it (and

Norman MacCaig in Bennet's Bar, Tollcross, Edinburgh, about 1981
(photo: Jessie Ann Matthew)

his kilt and the rigours of life at Balmoral)—the audience reacted with loud guffaws as he got to John Brown's final irritation in the shape of the 'sniggering gillies'.

Bach and the
18. Barbarians

MacCaig had three books of poetry published between 1977 and 1983. These are *Tree of Strings*, 1977, *The Equal Skies*, 1980, and *A World of Difference*, 1983.

They contain a lot of poetry in elegiac mood and there is much use of winter imagery in the poems about the death of A.K. (see earlier references to the poems to A.K. in Chapter 16). The poem 'In all that whiteness' contrasts the deadening effect of snow and ice with the warm, loving thoughts, like a 'glass of ruby wine' within the poet's own head. The feeling of winter is evocative not only of the time of year, but also of the time of life—the time when friends are dying.

There is also a continuation, if possible in even stronger vein, of the bitter 'anti-civilisation' poems of earlier volumes:

> When the barbarians came, things were better.
> They even let us wear our clothes
> when we went into the gas chambers.[1]

'Rewards and furies' about Columbus is similar in its vinegary tone:

> Columbus sailed and sailed and arrived.
> The poor soul didn't know where.
> Still, he succeeded:
> Indians were massacred, railways
> opened up wheatfields, jails and asylums,
> and skyscrapers walked around
> with atom bombs slung at their hips.

There is a sense in these bitter poems of someone pouring acid on to more acid. In 'No interims in history', the bitter cup is laced with black humour:

> *Barbarians!* growled Attila
> as the pile of skulls mounted higher.
> *What fun!* squealed Robespierre,
> shaking the gloved hand of Monsieur Guillotin...

> It would be good to think
> that Attila felt a headache coming on,
> that Monsieur Guillotin fingered the crick in his neck...

In several of the later poems MacCaig admits that he has difficulty in keeping his 'balance' in a world that offers him so many conflicting influences:

> ...I switch the radio
> from tortures in foreign prisons
> to a sonata of Schubert (that foreigner).
> I crawl from the swamp of nightmare into
> a glittering rainfall, a swathing of sunlight.
>
> Noticing you can do nothing about.
> It's the balancing that shakes my mind.
>
> What my friends don't notice
> is the weight of joy in my right hand
> and the weight of sadness in my left.
> All they see is MacCaig being upright,
> easy-oasy and jocose.[2]

On several occasions he mentions his own 'two faces'—the public, pleasant, smiling one and the other face which feels grief and compassion and fear and which he keeps hidden for most of the time. See, for example 'Private'.

There is also an increasing number of poems concerning death. MacCaig sees death as something alien and horrible, waiting round the corner to pounce on its victims and wrap them in their 'earthy coat'. An atheist, he sees death as the end, a full stop in existence, a going into 'nothingness'. 'Journeys' concerns the traverse from life to death:

> There are other bad journeys, to a bitter place
> I can't go to—yet. I lean towards it,
> tugging to get there, and thank God
> I'm clogged with the world. It grips me,
> I hold it.

In some of the later poems there are nightmarish references to an 'after life'. 'In that other world' depicts the dead sitting at a long table talking. In 'Old man in his chair' Death is a playboy waiting to come on stage—'capering and giggling yet again/at his one bad joke.' In 'Two skulls' the poet states:

> I hate death, the skull-maker, because he proves
> that destroying and making happen together.

—but then on a slightly more optimistic note he continues:

> He'll be no friend of mine, as long as I'm still
> a feathery pigeon or a scrapeskin dogfish.
>
> —I mean a man, whose skull contains
> ideas death never thought of.
>
> They'll cheat him, for they'll lodge in another skull
> —or become nothing, that comfortable absolute.

He had previously used this notion that 'ideas' escape death by moving from one skull to another at the end of 'Writers' Conference, Long Island University'.[3]

In 'Every day', MacCaig describes himself watching his own funeral, as if by Second Sight. The horse and cart drawing the body are ghosts, they turn into 'the field of slanted stones' and then

> My friends meet me. They lift me from the cart and,
> the greetings over, we go smiling underground.

He was actively atheistic, speaking out strongly against the idea of belief in an 'all powerful God'. But it is not only in these later poems that such feelings are found. There are throughout his work a certain number of 'railing at God' poems. 'Another flood' (*SS*) states:

> Too many doves have died, for us
> To be your image. Lightnings mark
> Only a bestial darkness round
> The pity of each floundering Ark.

MacCaig had a hatred of what he saw as the basic falseness of so much that goes on in the name of 'religion'; of the 'penny in the slot' responses which purveyors of religion demand.

MacCaig:

Many of the wars in society have been over religion. All sorts of totally ridiculous beliefs have been incorporated into Christianity. Christianity itself often contains warring sects (look at the history of England!)[4]

He claimed to be a rationalist and not to believe in 'pie in the sky'. He admitted he did not understand 'why we are here'. He had no idea why we have a universe and stars 'and no one else knows either', he said vehemently. He had a strong objection to the notion of faith, favouring the power of reason rather than the power of faith in a Supreme Being.

The poems in *A World of Difference* are very contemplative. The energy of the earlier poems has gone. There is a sad tone to many of them, a sense of flagging energy, of the inevitable onset of old age, and of disillusion with the world:

> Look at my hands—
> pickled like vegetables. Look at the secret crystals
> in my knee joints and shoulders. My eyelids' rims
> are drawn in blood, I stare at horizons
> through eyes bleached with salt other than theirs.[5]

But all is not of death and destruction. MacCaig had a tremendous love of music and referred to it particularly in these later poems. In the book *Tree of Strings* there are two poems about this—'Composers of music' and 'Down-to-earth heaven'. He said that if he could have been a composer, he would have preferred that to being a poet:

> Musicians...
> —I regard you with joy and with envy
> from my thicket of words.[6]

His taste in music was very catholic, and included fiddle music, bagpipe (mainly pibroch), harpsichord, organ, jazz, Mozart, Haydn, Bach, Scarlatti, Soler and Beethoven.

In 1981 he was interviewed on the radio by William Carrocher. During the rather argumentative and 'gritty' interview various pieces of music were played, chosen by MacCaig. The first was by Haydn and MacCaig spoke about his love of light-hearted music and also 'light' poetry:

MacCaig: I love music more than poetry in fact. That is to say, I respond to it more than poetry and I love all kinds of music but having a natural, I don't know, bias, weakness for laughing, although I love the great big heavy stuff, short of Mahler and Bruckner and those interminable bores, I do love when a great musician like Haydn gets into a larky mood, which I think he does here.
Carrocher: All right. It is Haydn's Piano Trio in A Major and it is played here by the Academy of Ancient Music, directed by Christopher Hogwood.

Music

Carrocher: Haydn in frivolous mood, in A Major...
MacCaig: (interjecting) I object to frivolous.
Carrocher: You object to frivolous?
MacCaig: Yes I do.
Carrocher: All right—light hearted.
MacCaig: Light hearted yes. This is a thing—I am sometimes accused of writing

frivolous poems and...

Carrocher: I would never so accuse you, sir.

MacCaig: Oh, well, you are a very nice polite chap I have never met before. Give you time, give you time! And do I not understand, people say, the world being what it is, with these fearful things going on in Cambodia and Chile, Ulster and England, Britain, that poetry should only be concerned with these large terrible matters and, of course, I think it should, but these large terrible matters have been going on all the time and yet poets and musicians don't mind painting a picture of two lemons and a guitar and a kipper or doing what Haydn just did and I also think that light music, light painting, light poetry can say very serious things in a beautifully indirect way. I don't like being preached at and clever boys like Beethoven, Haydn—these fellows, they say what they want to say without wagging an omnivorous and rapacious finger at you—you don't feel you are being devoured. So I like them.

The next piece of music in this programme was also fairly light.

MacCaig: It is a Bagatelle[7] by Mr Beethoven. Now it also is pretty larky as the Haydn one was but it has got a scale which has nothing to do with size that Haydn's did not have and it amazes and pleases me that Mr Beethoven calls it a Bagatelle.

MacCaig liked 'classical' as opposed to 'romantic' composers—preferring the precision, the mathematical accuracy, the vigour and optimism of Bach to the more diffuse meanderings of people like Wagner and Brahms. He did in fact see correlations between jazz and Bach. He introduced 'West End Blues' by Louis Armstrong, on the Carrocher programme:

MacCaig: I do love music, I truly do, in a huge wide range, including, for example, this one which is old jazz. It is a thing by Louis Armstrong and it starts with a cadenza on the trumpet that Mr Bach would have loved.

MacCaig also had a great love of harpsichord music and later in his interview with Carrocher he chose to hear one piece of such music:

MacCaig: It is an extraordinary piece[8] by a fellow called Soler who is a contemporary of Telemann and those chaps. I once heard of somebody saying in a derisory way of the harpsichord that it was like two skeletons copulating on a tin roof! O.K. let 'em hear this peculiar and extraordinary fandango.

Finally he chose a piece of violin music:

MacCaig: It is a violin sonata by a man called Ysaye and it is the most neurotic—as is clear I am a pragmatic kind of chap—but this is the most neurotic, spine-chilling piece of music I think that I know, beautifully played, extraordinarily played, by Oistrakh.[9]

In 'Moment musical in Assynt', MacCaig combines his love of music and his love of mountains—'A mountain is a sort of music'. Each of his favourite mountains in Assynt is likened to musical forms, ending with his favourite:

> I listen with my eyes and see through that
> Mellifluous din of shapes my masterpiece
> Of masterpieces:
> One sandstone chord that holds up time in space—
> Sforzando Suilven reared on his ground bass.

MacCaig was not influenced by music when writing his poems. If there was music playing while he was writing, he did not really 'hear' it.

A common feature of some of the later work is the use of a historical figure as the basis of the poem. In 'Folio' he makes fun of the characters of *Hamlet* in an anti-romantic, anti-tragic way, describing them as they could have been, before Shakespeare got hold of them.

> Shakespeare who
>
> will translate all this
> into gothic glooms and ghosts and garrulities.

He seems to be saying, as in the later poem 'John Brown and Queen Victoria'— 'The historical figure may seem all very grand and dramatic but was he (or she) really like that?'

19. | Edinburgh Again

In later life MacCaig was the recipient of several honours. In 1979 he was made an Officer of the Order of the British Empire. In 1981 he became the Royal Scottish Academy's new Professor of Literature, elected to this honorary post in place of Hugh MacDiarmid. In this year also, he was awarded an honorary doctorate by Stirling University. In 1983, on the occasion of the 400th anniversary of the founding of Edinburgh University, he received the degree of Doctor of Letters and in 1986 he was awarded the Queen's Medal for Poetry. This award was instituted in 1933 by George V and this was only the twenty-fourth time that the medal was awarded. Later that year he was awarded the honorary degree of Doctor of Laws at Dundee University.

In August 1985 his *Collected Poems*[1] was published by Chatto and Windus, and in November 1985 it was named as 'Scottish Book of the Year' in the Royal Bank of Scotland/Saltire Society literary awards.

On 18 November 1985, in the Georgian elegance of the Queen's Hall, Edinburgh, a 75th Birthday Party was held for him. On roads from 'a' the airts' came the poets, the writers and the friends of a lifetime—Iain Crichton Smith, Sorley MacLean, Edwin Morgan, Seamus Heaney, Liz Lochhead, Alexander Scott, Ishbel MacLean, Adam MacNaughtan, John Herdman, Valerie Gillies, Alasdair Macrae, Roderick Watson, Valda MacDiarmid, David Campbell, Emilio Coia and many, many others.

At little candlelit tables at the front of the hall sat the elect, a group of famous faces. MacCaig sat at the edge of the group, thin, tall, white-haired, puffing cigarettes.

The poets and the musicians one by one paid tribute to him and read poetry and prose or sang. Seamus Heaney and Adam MacNaughton read poems specially written for him.

The friendship with Heaney which started in Edinburgh in 1973 was to grow and flourish. Heaney relates:

Marie and I would visit him and his beloved Isabel in their apartment in Leamington Terrace, at that fireside where the poems got written, the music got played and the life got examined, day by day, line by line, cigarette by cigarette. Then as the years went on, our friendship deepened, the banter and blarney kept going, the vying and the playing stayed true, and I learnt that this was one of the best things life has to offer, the joy of being able to love and respect the poet as much as the poetry.[2]

In 1988 *Voice Over* was published. In this book there is a mood of gentleness. A lot of the poems repeat ideas and themes of the past. But there are still some of strange originality, breaking the mould again of past poems. One such is 'Neighbour'. Reminiscent of one of the characters in a Jacques Tati film, the neighbour appears to be an automaton, living out a life timed to perfection.

> What does he do at home? Sit at attention?
> Or does he stay in the lobby
> like a hatstand?
>
> Does his wife know she married
> a diagram? That she goes to bed
> with a faded blueprint?

Perhaps this is a comment on the futility of modern city life with its clock-watching, its rigid routines, its superficial relationships and its de-humanising effect.

In 'Compare and contrast' he discusses a great thinker spending forty years attempting to penetrate 'the dark forest of ideas' and points rather cheekily to the fact that the common hen can do better. It can find its nest in a field of oats with nothing more than its own inbuilt radar system!

During her later years Isabel suffered from cancer. She was ill for a time and then had a two year remission. In *Voice Over* MacCaig's concern for her is evident in the poems 'Her illness' and 'End of her illness'. As in 'Visiting hour' the poet is recalling feelings of great intensity and stress. He has come through 'cloudy months' haunted by fear that his wife would die, but she did not, and the effect is that:

> ...the whole air is a music I can hardly hear
> but hear all the time.

However, the cancer recurred and, sadly and inevitably, she died in 1990.

She left an immense gap in MacCaig's life. A very gifted woman in the field of English literature, she was in fact a very unassuming person who tended to be in the background of his public life, not seeking the limelight. And yet she smoothed the tracks, fed his friends, plied callers with coffee and was frequently consulted for confirmation of details during interviews. While MacCaig was talking to all-comers in the sitting room, she would be quietly preparing the fish for the lunch. It was she who drove him to poetry readings—and dropped him off at the door. To say that Isabel shunned the limelight is the mildest of understatements!

David Campbell, the writer and broadcaster, visited MacCaig in November 1990 a few months after Isabel's death and gives us a fairly comic view of the literary lion in his den. When Campbell arrived MacCaig was preparing lunch for them both.

Isabel MacCaig at Hazel Goodsir Smith's house in 1978
(photo: Hazel Goodsir Smith)

Campbell:

Then he tells us:—'I can't cook.' To illustrate the point, two eggs are already burning, the extent of his culinary expertise! He hadn't remembered I was bringing a pal, the photographer Robin Gillanders, so I add an egg to the boiling water, which ignites a furious flyting about my cooking ineptitude, submitting a cold egg to boiling water! 'The water should start cold.' We are at once at home and to his dramatic chagrin my egg is perfect—something he will doubtless dispute, now that it is boldly in print.

Campbell talks about Isabel's death:

Palpably, though, one feels in the house the absence of Norman's wife, Isabel, who died earlier this year. She was a noted scholar and lexicographer; and now, her intuitive supply of remarks or tea at just the right moment are gone. Inevitably the conversation begins here. MacCaig: 'After Isabel's death I was rescued by my family, by my daughter Joan and her husband Jim, and by my son Ewen. I'd be a miserable old beggar apart from them and my two granddaughters. And friends are very important to me as well.'

Asked by Campbell about his work, and particularly about the readings he was doing, MacCaig said:

I'm too busy. I've a deformity of the throat that prevents me from saying 'No'. But I haven't written a poem this year. Isabel suffered so much, poetry seemed trivial. I think it's a permanent blockage. Maybe not, you never know. It's sad, isn't it. I wish I could. It's another absence as well as hers.[3]

On 14 November 1990, an 80th Birthday Party was held for MacCaig, again in the Queen's Hall. There was a tremendous buzz about the place. The normally restrained Edinburgh concert goers were replaced by literati of all shades of opinion, folk singers, musicians, friends and colleagues. Drifting in with the crowd came Sorley MacLean, Iain Crichton Smith, Aly Bain (the virtuoso Scottish fiddler), Adam MacNaughtan, Liz Lochhead, Dolina MacLennan, Brian MacCabe, Tom Pow and Seamus Heaney.

While everyone was arriving, Norman, puffing at cigarettes as usual, stood quietly in the bar chatting mildly and nursing a 'Grouse'.

The event had a sense of family celebration about it. These people were friends, not just an audience. When MacCaig got onto the platform at the start, everyone stood spontaneously to applaud him. His first greeting was schoolmasterly. 'Sit down', he said, reprovingly.

David Campbell recalls:

In England they confer knighthoods. In Scotland a small élite have been made life members of the Scotch Malt Whisky Society. At this birthday presentation, its chairman, Pip Hills, conferred this honour on the poet with a case of the best, to which the recipient drily responded: 'A life membership for a man of 80!'[4]

In the early 1990s MacCaig was asked to do a great many poetry readings in schools, universities and elsewhere. The study of a selection of his poems was made part of the syllabus for the Scottish Revised Higher English examinations at this time.

In 1992, during the Edinburgh Festival, an event was organised in the Traverse Theatre in Edinburgh. At this MacCaig was in conversation with Aly Bain, the Shetland fiddler. MacCaig read his poems and Bain played his fiddle.

He and Bain had first met in the early 1970s when Bain was about 25. Bain has achieved fame throughout the world for his extraordinary playing. Billy Connolly, the comedian and one-time folk musician, has described him at a folk club in Glasgow:

And there was Aly, straight from Shetland, in a wee V-necked pullover and a wee shirt. And he just blew everyone away. I had never heard a fiddle played like that before. I had never heard the clarity of tone or the volume from a fiddle before. I had never heard that *passion* on a fiddle.[5]

The Traverse event got under way. Bain is a slow-talking 'careful how you put it' sort of man. He and MacCaig were obviously following some sort of script they had in their heads, but it appeared that MacCaig was deviating from his part of the script. For instance on one occasion Bain fed him a carefully phrased question about MacDiarmid, evidently supposed to release a flow of talk from MacCaig. All MacCaig said was 'No'. Sniggers from the audience. Bain: 'Well, *elaborate!*' And a general laugh all round. The evening was full of quips and wisecracks.

Bain: When did you begin playing the fiddle, Norman?
MacCaig: Half past nine in the morning. It was raining. It was a Thursday.
(Laughter)

Towards the end of the evening Bain and MacCaig got onto the engrossing subject of frogs.

Bain: Norman has written a few poems about frogs and this is the last one...
MacCaig: A lot of people rather like these poems and I can well imagine when I die and I am spoken about for a *fortnight* say, somebody will say, 'Do you remember that fellow, MacCaig?' And the other one would say, 'Oh, aye, the frog poet?' And I did not want to be hurtling through that fortnight of immortality as 'the frog poet', so I decided I would stop.

My last word on frogs[6]

People have said to me, *You seem to like frogs.*
They keep jumping into your poems.

I do. I love the way they sit,
compact as a cat and as indifferent
to everything but style, like a lady remembering
to keep her knees together. And I love
the elegant way they jump and
the inelegant way they land.
So human.

I feel so close to them
I must be froggish myself.
I look in the mirror expecting to see
a fairytale Prince.

But no. It's just sprawling me,
croaking away
and swivelling my eyes around
for the stealthy heron and his stabbing beak.

The general feeling at this performance was of warmth. As Aly Bain said, half way through: 'This is going to be a mutual admiration society all night, except when we fall out which could happen at any time.'

MacCaig continued to go up to Lochinver after Isabel's death, with Joan, her husband Jim MacLean and their daughters, for short holidays of two or three weeks, living in a quiet croft house mid-way between Lochinver and Achmelvich.

In 1993 he had a slight stroke, whose only effect was that his writing became ugly and illegible and he had to dictate letters to someone else.

Latterly he developed problems with walking. At an interview in August 1995 he said:

I am crippled so I don't get out much. I depend on friends with motor cars and, of course, family. They visit me a lot. Thank goodness. I cannot walk any distance.[7]

His son, Ewen, called often and cooked for the two of them, and he went out frequently to his daughter's home for a meal with her and her family. Playing the grandfatherly role was now MacCaig's forté. MacCaig: 'All my descendants, my daughter, her husband, two grand daughters, my son, are all far, far cleverer than I am'.[8]

One grand daughter, Catherine, was at this time writing a PhD on life in Assynt— how the area has changed and developed over the years.

When at home, MacCaig read a lot and watched television. His favourite TV was

Norman MacCaig and Aly Bain in the Tron Tavern, Edinburgh
(photo: Gordon Thomson)

anything on animals and birds, particularly if it was a programme by David Attenborough.

On 22 November 1995, an 85th Birthday Party was held for MacCaig in the Assembly Rooms in George Street. This took place in the main ballroom, a hall which is hung about with enormous, glittering chandeliers. A platform had been placed along one side of the hall and there is a gallery on the other side. Underneath this gallery a bar had been set up. MacCaig sat near the platform with friends, but did not take part in the readings.

A vast crowd turned up. One of the surprising things about this event was the large number of young people present. The readers included Douglas Dunn, Sorley MacLean, Iain Crichton Smith, Valerie Gillies, Hamish Henderson, Alasdair Gray and many other readers, singers and musicians.

The evening finished with a performance by Aly Bain and his band the Boys of the Lough, at which Bain played some electrifying solo fiddle music in tribute to Norman. As Joy Hendry wrote in the *Scotsman* after MacCaig's death:

> Music probably mattered more to him than anything else, witness his great bond with fiddler Aly Bain. The most poignant moment of the 85th birthday came at the end, when most people had left. Aly came over to Norman's table, emotionally trying to say something meaningful: Norman fixed him with a beady eye and said: 'Play me something, boy!' Aly obeyed, leaning towards Norman, his fiddle caressing out an unbearably beautiful slow air, and to us, observing from the next table, the two seemed to merge into one.[9]

Until the end of 1995 he lived alone in his old, traditional-type flat in the Polwarth area of Edinburgh. Visitors found a house which was sparsely furnished—in fact the entrance hall was large and almost completely empty. The sitting room was comfortable if rather plain with dark settee and armchairs, small tables and, towering around one, tier upon tier of books on two walls. Another wall contained windows looking out onto a side street and the fourth, fireplace wall, was covered in pictures of scenes and friends from the past—MacDiarmid sporting his pipe amid scenes from Assynt and Italy. MacCaig had his own chair which he regarded as his by territorial right and in which he normally sat. Most of his poetry was written in this bookish, rather doucely furnished room. A tape recorder stood nearby and was played a great deal. Outside the window, in a garden across the street, stood a beautiful pear tree—a fairly fruitless one according to MacCaig. In fact it caused a stir in the neighbourhood once by producing one pear! The leafy branches and the changing sky outside, and the narrow side street with its ever-restless traffic were his only view.

In late 1995 MacCaig was becoming very frail and his memory was becoming very unreliable. At New Year he had a bad fall and was so affected by this that he was taken into the Edinburgh Royal Infirmary. His health deteriorated rapidly and he died in the Astley Ainslie Hospital on 23 January 1996.

Numerous obituaries and appreciations were published during the ensuing days in the newspapers—in *The Times*, the *Guardian*, the *Scotsman* (three or four over several days), the *Herald*, the *Daily Telegraph* and the *Independent*.

The funeral at Warriston Crematorium in Edinburgh was held on Monday 29 January. The main chapel was packed out with friends, relatives, academics, writers and media people. The funeral started with the singing of the psalm 'I to the hills will lift mine eyes, from whence doth come mine aid'.

Thereafter various people contributed. Alasdair Macrae of Stirling University gave a warm tribute to Norman as a personality, sketching for us a tough, humorous character, who enjoyed nothing better than a good-going argument with friends. Adam MacNaughtan read some of MacCaig's poems, particularly the vivid 'Return to Scalpay' and a poem for A.K. MacLeod, 'Praise of a man', which on this occasion was used as a memorial for MacCaig himself:

> He went through a company like a lamplighter—
> see the dull minds, one after another,
> begin to glow, to shed
> a beneficent light.

Ishbel MacAskill sang two Gaelic songs and Norman MacAskill, a long-time friend from Lochinver, recounted memories of MacCaig on his holidays in Assynt.

The proceedings closed with tape recordings of music played by Aly Bain (who was unable to attend as he was giving a concert in Germany). Bain played first a slow air on the fiddle and then concluded with a reel. During the reel everyone stood and the family left, followed by the assembled throng, and went out into the cold January air and into a crowd of mourners waiting to get in (late) for the next funeral.

Those present had been invited to adjourn after the funeral to the Traverse Theatre Bar—considering MacCaig's views, a highly appropriate place for a post-funeral gathering.

All his life MacCaig had a strong antipathy to the idea of writing articles about himself and his life. He was a poet who went in for a great deal of self-deprecation, frequently to the bafflement of interviewers who were intent on promoting his image as one of Scotland's foremost poets. Alistair Moffat, towards the end of a TV interview in 1982, said to him: 'Have you ever thought of writing an autobiography, reporting on all of your life?'

To which MacCaig replied: 'No. It would last…if I spun it out…it would be about a page and a half.'[10]

Trying to discuss his work is rather like trying to discuss the sea. One can put a small amount of MacCaig onto a page or one can observe the sea on a calm day from the shore, then say 'that is MacCaig' or 'that is sea water'. There is no way, however, that one can accurately measure and indicate the turbulence, the varying aspects, the storms, the cruel wit, the subtle jokes, the moments of depression, the visions of love, the everyday clarity or the mysterious depths of his poetry. Like the changes in the moods of the sea, it defies description. The more one rationalises and analyses and attempts to confine and explain MacCaig, the more he runs off, hides round the corner and jumps out in another guise. For he writes in many styles and moods and on themes as diverse as humanity itself.

Despite the wide range of his output, he is yet distinctive. He has a voice of his own which sets him apart from any other poet—something to do with his wit, his precision and his brevity. He is a mixture of Gaelic and Edinburgh 'bourgeois', but it is the Gaelic element which predominates.

He will never write his autobiography, but his poems will be there to glimmer with mysterious fire: gifts for those who follow him.

Notes

Chapter One

1   Norman MacCaig altered the spelling from McCaig to MacCaig for literary purposes
2   From 'Aunt Julia'
3   From 'Return to Scalpay'
4   'Wreck'
5   See 'Uncle Roderick'
6   Interview MacCaig/McNeill
7   From 'Uncle Seamus'
8   'Aunt Julia'
9   From 'A man in Assynt'
10   'Autobiographical Note' (unpublished?). Read aloud by MacCaig during an interview with Alistair Moffat on 'Encore' on S.T.V., 3 June 1982
11   *Schola Regia*, Summer 1927, p.48
12   *Schola Regia*, Easter 1928, p.124
13   *Schola Regia*, Summer 1928, pp.154-5
14   *Ibid.*, pp.163-6
15   *Ibid.*, pp.157-8

Chapter Two

1   Interview on 'The Slice', Radio Scotland, between Edi Stark and MacCaig on 16 July 93
2   A series of variations on a theme for bagpipe
3   There is a recording in the School of Scottish Studies, Edinburgh, of MacCaig playing pibroch on the fiddle
4   From 'Piper in the Dark' in *Penguin Modern Poets, 21*, published about 1971-2.
5   *Schola Regia*, Easter, 1932
6   A Teacher Training College in Edinburgh
7   A.T.Tolley, *Poetry of the Thirties*, 1975, p.365
8   Published in *Chapman* 16, Summer 1976, p.3
9   5 September 1948.Thomas and Evans belonged to a group of poets, readers and

musicians who called themselves 'The Apollo Society' and who did perform-
ances of poetry and music

Chapter Three

1 This and several following extracts from MacCaig's wartime recollections in
   Voices from War ed. Ian MacDougall, 1995, p.283
2 Detention
3 A conscientious objector
4 A notorious Scottish prison
5 MacDougall, *op. cit.*, p.284
6 Interview MacCaig/McNeill
7 *Ibid.*
8 MacDougall, *op. cit.*, p.284
9 *Ibid.*, p.287
10 *Ibid.*, p.288
11 Interview MacLean/McNeill, 1984

Chapter Four

1 See 'A man in Assynt'
2 From 'Stonechat on Cul Beg'
3 From 'Above Inverkirkaig'
4 See 'Toad'
5 See 'Remembering old Murdo scything'
6 From 'Clachtoll'

Chapter Five

1 From 'The Vision of the Prodigal Son' by Sydney Goodsir Smith
2 In 'Tom Scott in the Fifties', *Scotia Review* No. 13-14 (Tom Scott Double
   Issue), November 1976
3 Radio Scotland, 14 November 1980
4 *Ibid.*
5 Alasdair Gray, *1982 Janine*, 1984
6 Interview MacCaig/McNeill
7 From Alan Bold, 'Bards at the bar: a toast to "the poets' pub"', *Scotsman* 17
   June 1984
8 From a description by George Mackay Brown of Milne's Bar in the fifties
   written at the request of McNeill and sent to her with a letter of 28 January
   1983
9 George Mackay Brown interviewed by Jeremy Bruce-Watt in the *Scotsman*,
   February 1983
10 Bold, 'Bards at the bar'
11 MacCaig's home in Edinburgh

12 George Mackay Brown's description of Milne's Bar, see note 8 above
13 Hugh MacDiarmid, *The Company I've Kept*, 1966, p.161
14 *Ibid.*, pp.72-3
15 Mackay Brown, *op. cit.*
16 'The Norman Conquest', *Voice of Scotland* vol. 6, no.2, July 1955, p.17
17 The *Scotsman*, 1 June 1957
18 From Peter Butter, *Edwin Muir: Man and Poet*, 1966
19 *Honour'd Shade*, ed. Norman MacCaig, 1959

Chapter Six

1 A district of Edinburgh
2 Hugh MacDiarmid, *The Company I've Kept*, 1966, p.235
3 From 'Traffic stop'
4 An area of the Water of Leith near Warriston where there were lots of 'puddocks' (Scots word for frogs)
5 See Chapter 14, p.88
6 Karl Miller, 'Romantic Town' in *Memoirs of a Modern Scotland*, ed. Karl Miller, 1970

Chapter Seven

1 From 'A good day', *RA*, 1962
2 See later material on the 'holy' poems in Chapter 9, pp.60-1
3 M.H. Abrams, *A Glossary of Literary Terms*, 1971, p.92
4 'Neoclassical MacCaig' by Mary Jane W. Scott in *Studies in Scottish Literature* X, 3 (January 1973) ed. G. Ross Roy, p.137
5 From 'Peter Quince at the Clavier'
6 Chapter on Wallace Stevens by W.Y. Tindall in *Seven Modern American Poets —An Introduction*, ed. Leon Unger, 1967
7 *Ibid.*
8 From 'Tea At the Palaz of Noon'
9 Christopher Grieve (Hugh MacDiarmid)
10 Interview of 3 June 1982, on 'Encore', STV

Chapter Eight

1 From 'A. K.'s summer hut'
2 Interview MacCaig/McNeill
3 From 'A man in Assynt'

Chapter Nine

1 See 'Summer Farm'
2 From 'A man in Assynt'
3 See 'High up on Suilven'

Chapter Ten

1 'My way of it' in *Chapman* 16, Summer 1976
2 Interview of 3 June 1982, on 'Encore', STV
3 See also Chapter 6, p.40
4 Interview MacCaig/McNeill
5 *Ibid.*
6 From 'Last night in New York'
7 This was changed to '...the hush-hush language of grass' in *CP*
8 Interview MacCaig/McNeill
9 Extra material was added in *CP*
10 Maurice Lindsay, *History of Scottish Literature*, 1977, p.402
11 Interview of 1981, in 'Carrocher in Conversation', BBC. See also Chapter 18, pp.114-5

Chapter Eleven

1 Edinburgh *Evening News*, 7 August 1968
2 Letter to McNeill of 24 April 1984
3 Interview MacCaig/Roderick Watson, Radio Scotland, 14 November 1980
4 Interview MacCaig/McNeill
5 This took place 4 September 1969
6 Interview MacCaig/McNeill
7 This poem appears in *Collected Poems* (1985) but the fourth, fifth and sixth lines were omitted in error. This was corrected in the 1990 edition of *Collected Poems*
8 Nancy Gish, *Hugh MacDiarmid: The Man and His Work*, 1984, p.68

Chapter Twelve

1 From 'One way journey'
2 'Vestey's Well'
3 'Hill being organ' (*M*, not in *CP*)
4 'Moon'
5 'The Pass of the Roaring'
6 E.g. 'Hill being organ' (*M*, not in *CP*), 'Moment musical in Assynt', 'Above Inverkirkaig', 'No accident'
7 'Spate in winter midnight'
8 See Chapter 7, p.43
9 For example, 'July landing' and 'Culag pier'
10 See 'Gulls on a hill loch', 'Rhu Mor', 'Cormorants nesting' and 'Puffin'
11 From 'Culag pier'
12 'In everything'
13 'Praise of a boat'
14 See 'Culag pier' and 'Midnight, Lochinver'
15 By this time owned by Scandinavian Property Services (U.K.) Ltd.

Chapter Thirteen
1   Interview Macrae/McNeill

Chapter Fourteen
1   Seamus Heaney, 'A poet remembered': article in the *Scotsman*, 27 January 1996
2   An Irish traditional instrumental group
3   A popular seventeenth century poet. His verse is generally considered to be lightweight
4   Heaney, 'A poet remembered'
5   In 'Bards at the bar: a toast to "the poet's pub"', *Scotsman*, 17 June 1984
6   The *Orcadian*, 15 April 1971
7   Introduction to *Seven New Voices*, 1972
8   *Scotsman*, 1 November 1980
9   From an article by Michael Aitken, 'Norman MacCaig: best Scottish poet writing in English', *Scotsman,* 19 June 1976
10 At the Netherbow, Edinburgh

Chapter Fifteen
1   Seamus Heaney, 'A poet remembered': article in the *Scotsman*, 27 January 1996
2   Erik Frykman, *Unemphatic Marvels: A Study of Norman MacCaig's Poetry, Gothenburg Studies in English 35*, Gotenborg, Sweden, 1977
3   Interview MacCaig/McNeill
4   While he was away during War-time, Isabel MacCaig sent some of his early poems to Routledge and Kegan Paul and they were published (see Chapter 2)
5   Interview on the Radio Scotland series 'The Slice' between Edi Stark and MacCaig on 16 July 1993

Chapter Sixteen
1   From 'An Elegy upon the Death of Mistress Boulstred'
2   Radio Scotland interview with Roderick Watson, 14 November 1980
3   See 'A.K. MacLeod'
4   From 'A month after his death'
5   From 'Triple burden'
6   *Scotsman*, 15 August 1977
7   *Scotsman*, 14 September 1978
8   'The Little White Rose'

Chapter Seventeen
1   *So Many Summers*, Stirling University, 1978 (limited edition)
2   A district of Edinburgh

3   Edinburgh *Evening News,* 23 March 1977, 'Doing the right thing by Norman MacCaig'
4   Erik Frykman, *Unemphatic Marvels: A Study of Norman MacCaig's Poetry, Gothenburg Studies in English 35*, Gotenborg, Sweden, 1977
5   *Northern Studies* 10, 1971
6   Writer and lecturer at Stirling University
7   See also Chapter 4
8   *Seven Poets*, Third Eye Centre, Glasgow, 1981
9   *Scots Magazine,* September, 1981
10 *Edinburgh Review*, Summer 1981

Chapter Eighteen

1   From 'A new age'
2   From 'Equilibrist'
3   See Chapter 10
4   Interview MacCaig/McNeill
5   From 'Fisherman'
6   From 'Composers of music'
7   Bagatelle No. 5 in C Major
8   Soler's 'Fandango'
9   B.B.C. interview 'Carrocher in Conversation', 1981

Chapter Nineteen

1   See note on this and the 1990 edition of *Collected Poems* in the Introduction, p.x
2   Seamus Heaney, 'A poet remembered': article in the *Scotsman*, 27 January 1996
3   David Campbell, article in the *Scotsman*, 14 November 1990
4   *Ibid.*
5   In Alastair Clark, *Fiddler on the Loose*, 1993, p.127
6   'My last word on frogs' was written about 1983
7   Interview MacCaig/McNeill
8   *Ibid.*
9   29 January 1996
10 On the programme 'Encore' (see Chapter 17, p.108)

Bibliography

Books of poetry by Norman MacCaig

Far Cry, Routledge and Kegan Paul, 1943
The Inward Eye, Routledge and Kegan Paul, 1946
Riding Lights, The Hogarth Press, 1955
The Sinai Sort, The Hogarth Press, 1957
A Common Grace, Chatto and Windus, 1960
A Round of Applause, Chatto and Windus, 1962
Measures, Chatto and Windus, 1965
Surroundings, Chatto and Windus, 1966
Rings on a Tree, Chatto and Windus, 1968
A Man in My Position, Chatto and Windus, 1969
Selected Poems, The Hogarth Press, 1971
The White Bird, Chatto and Windus, 1973
The World's Room, Chatto and Windus, 1974
Tree of Strings, Chatto and Windus, 1977
Old Maps and New: Selected Poems, The Hogarth Press, 1978
The Equal Skies, Chatto and Windus, 1980
A World of Difference, Chatto and Windus, 1983
Collected Poems, Chatto and Windus, 1985
Voice-Over, Chatto and Windus, 1988
Collected Poems, A New Edition, Chatto and Windus, 1990

Articles and chapters in books by MacCaig

'Stevenson the Traveller', *Schola Regia*, Summer 1928
'By Loch Assynt and Loch Crocach', *Listener*, 14 November 1968
'A Note on the Author', introduction to Hugh MacDiarmid, *Scottish Eccentrics*, 1972
'My Way of It', *Chapman* 16, Summer 1976
Chapter about his wartime experiences in *Voices from War*, ed. Ian MacDougall, 1995

Books about MacCaig and his poetry

Erik Frykman, *Unemphatic Marvels: A Study of Norman MacCaig's Poetry, Gothenburg Studies in English 35*, Gotenborg, Sweden, 1977

Norman MacCaig, Critical Essays, ed. Joy Hendry and Raymond Ross, Edinburgh University Press, 1990

Chapter in *Seven Poets*, Third Eye Centre, Glasgow, 1981. This also contains paintings by Alexander Moffat and photographs by Jessie Ann Matthew of MacCaig

So Many Summers, Stirling University, 1978 (limited edition volume presented to MacCaig on his leaving Stirling University)

Roderick Watson, *The Poetry of Norman MacCaig, Scotnotes No. 5*, Association for Scottish Literary Studies, 1989

Book of poems presented to MacCaig

Norman MacCaig—A Celebration, Chapman, 1995. Presented on the occasion of his 85th birthday

Index

1; Edinburgh Castle 16; Edinburgh Royal Infirmary 124; Freemasons' Hall 15; General Post Office 40; Grange 36; Grassmarket 36, 38; Hanover Street 39; High Street 36; Howard Place 34; Liberton 84; Marchmont 104; Netherbow 93; New Town Hotel 89; Polwarth 36, 124; Princes Street 41, 59; 'Puddocky' 36; Queen's Hall 117, 120; Reid School of Music 92; Rose Street 27, 30, 38-9, 91; Royal Mile 41; South Queensferry 74; Tollcross 36; Traverse Theatre 121, 125; Union Canal 36, 39; Warriston Crematorium 125; Water of Leith 36

Edinburgh Education Authority 18

Edinburgh Evening Dispatch 40

Edinburgh Festival 15, 121

Edinburgh Ladies College 9

Edinburgh University 12, 71-7, 117

Edinburgh University Classical Society 9-10

Eliot, T.S. 71

Elphin 79, 106

Evans, Dame Edith 15

Ferlinghetti, Lawrence 84

Films of Scotland Committee 105

First World War 16

Florence 40

Free Church 4

Freud, Sigmund 13

Frost, Robert 84

Frykman, Erik 96, 105

Garioch, Robert 26, 33, 39, 88, 91, 92, 107

Gillanders, Robin 120

Gillies, Valerie 71, 80, 117, 124

Ginsberg, Allen 84

Gish, Nancy 75

Glen Canisp 59

Glen, Duncan 91

Grant, 'Puggy' 6

Graves, Robert 63

Gray, Alasdair 25, 124,

Green, Stanley Roger 24, 33, 92

Grieve, Christopher *see* MacDiarmid, Hugh

Gunn, Neil 30, 105

Hamburg 17

Haydn, Franz Joseph 8, 114-5

Harris (island of) 1, 4, 98

Harris, O.K. 108

Haugh of Urr 1

Heaney, Marie 117

Heaney, Seamus 89-90, 95, 117, 120

Hebrides 98

Henderson, Hamish 4, 124

Hendry, Joy 124

Herbert, George 84

Herdman, John 88, 93, 117

Heretics, the 88-9 91, 92, 93

Herrick, Robert 90

Hills, Pip 121

Hitler, Adolf 19

Hogwood, Christopher 114

Holub, Miroslav 84

H.M.S. Pinafore 7

Hogarth Press 27

Hopkins, Gerard Manley, 'Inversnaid' 29

Inchnadamph 21

Inverkirkaig 21, 50, 58, 82, 101, 102

Inveruplan 51, 52, 54-5, 58-9

Italy 40, 65, 124

Kay, Ada 89

Kennish, Lannette 71-2

Kilkenny 90

King Kong 68

King Gillies, W. 6

Kitaj, R.B. 107

'Lament for the Children' (pibroch) 103

Lamont, Willie 25

Langholm cemetery 103

L'Aquila, Italy 40

Lawrie, Hamish 98

Leigh, David 92

Lewis (island of) 4

Li Po 52

Lindsay, Maurice 13, 69

Linklater, Eric 105

Littlewood, Mark 105

Loch an Ordain 57

Loch Assynt 78

Loch Bad a Ghaill 21

Loch Lurgainn 20

Lochhead, Liz 93, 108, 117, 120

NORMAN MACCAIG

NORMAN MACCAIG

NORMAN MACCAIG

NORMAN MACCAIG

NORMAN MACCAIG

NORMAN MACCAIG

NORMAN MACCAIG

NORMAN MACCAIG

NORMAN MACCAIG

NORMAN MACCAIG

NORMAN MACCAIG

NORMAN MACCAIG

NORMAN MACCAIG

NORMAN MACCAIG

NORMAN MACCAIG

NORMAN MACCAIG

NORMAN MACCAIG

NORMAN MACCAIG

NORMAN MACCAIG

Split Rock 21, 22
Stac Pollaidh 20-1
Stalin, Joseph 19
Stark, Edi 10, 99-100
Stevens, Wallace 47, 62, 84, 98
Stirling University 84-7, 104, 117
Strathan 21
Stoer 21, 52
Student, The (Edinburgh University
    magazine) 10
Suilven 21, 58, 59, 60, 78, 79, 116
Surrealism 13, 14

Telemann, Georg Philipp 115
Third Eye Centre, Glasgow 107
1320 Club, Edinburgh 73
Thomas, Dylan 13, 15, 29
Thomson, Derick 33
Tindall, W.Y. 47
Tolley, A.T. 13
Toulouse-Lautrec, Henri de 67
Tranströmer, Tomas 84
Treece, Henry 13
Tremayne, Sydney 33

Ullapool 20

Van Gogh 30, 44
Vestey, Lord 82
Voznesenski, Andrei 84

Wagner, Richard 115
Watkins, Vernon 13
Watson, Roderick 24, 25, 72, 88, 117
Watt, Bob 26, 27, 91
The Way I Say It (record) 90
Westminster 64
Weston, Professor John 68
White Goddess 99
Wicklow 89, 90
Williams, William Carlos 84
Wilson, Marjorie 107
Writers' Conference, New York 65, 67, 68

Yeats, W.B. 31, 70, 99
Young, Douglas 24, 25, 26
Ysaye, Eugene 115